THE
TWITTER
HISTORY OF
THE WORLD

GW00597992

Kelvin MacKenzie and Chas Newkey-Burden

THE
TWITTER
HISTORY OF
THE WORLD

Everything you need to know about everything
in 140 characters or less

JOHN BLAKE

Published by John Blake Publishing Ltd,
3 Bramber Court, 2 Bramber Road,
London W14 9PB, England

www.johnblakepublishing.co.uk

www.facebook.com/Johnblakepub   facebook

twitter.com/johnblakepub   twitter

First published in paperback in 2012

ISBN: 978-1-85782-822-1

British Library Cataloguing-in-Publication Data:

A catalogue record for this book is available from the British Library.

Design by www.envydesign.co.uk

Printed in Great Britain by CPI Group (UK) Ltd

1 3 5 7 9 10 8 6 4 2

© Text copyright Chas Newkey-Burden and Kelvin MacKenzie 2012

Papers used by John Blake Publishing are natural, recyclable products
made from wood grown in sustainable forests. The manufacturing
processes conform to the environmental regulations of the country
of origin.

Every attempt has been made to contact the relevant copyright-holders,
but some were unobtainable. We would be grateful if the appropriate
people could contact us.

Historians are gossips who tease the dead.
(@Voltaire)

Follow the authors on Twitter:

Kelvin MacKenzie: @MacKenzieKelvin
Chas Newkey-Burden: @AllThatChas

All 'tweets' in this book are the authors'.
They are fictional and do not necessarily
represent actual tweets. Any connection with
such tweets appearing on Twitter is purely
coincidental. This book is not official Twitter
merchandise and has not been authorised
by Twitter.

THE WORLD IS CREATED

@God
Been working like a dog for six days creating heaven + earth. Getting the firmaments right was a bitch. Enough already – DM if you need me.
11.59pm, 6 January, 0000

Whether you believe in the big bang theory, or that God created the world in six days, this page represents the day the universe started. This is 'Tweet zero'.

ADAM & EVE

@God
Awesome: @Adam has got a Twitter account, so I'll be able to keep an eye on him and @Eve. Guys, don't eat from the Tree of Knowledge.
8.12am, 9 January, 0000

@Serpent
@Adam @Eve Don't listen to him. Eat from the tree of knowledge all you like. What happens in Eden stays in Eden.
11.44am, 9 January, 0000

@Eve
Wow, the fruit from that tree is #Nom! @Adam had some too. We're both rocking the fig leaf look now. Does my bum look big in this?
2.21pm, 9 January, 0000

@God
@Adam @Eve Erm, remember I follow you guys on Twitter. I saw what you did – you guys are sooo in the crap now.
2.24pm, 9 January, 0000

@Adam
#FML
2.26pm, 9 January, 0000
[Retweeted by @Eve]

This mini-saga of a man, a woman, a snake and a tree is filled with symbolism in the eyes of some religions.

NOAH AND THE FLOOD

@Noah
As if the weather forecast said there was only a 40% chance of rain! Who's even running this show?
11.48am, 12 March, 0000

@DisgustedofTunbridgeWells
I know, right? All this rain but do they cancel the hosepipe ban? Like heck they do – tut!
11.49am, 12 March, 0000

@Noah
It's biblical correctness gone mad. Ah well, best get gathering some animals for the #ark.
11.52am, 12 March, 0000

According to the book of Genesis, Noah saved himself, his family and a whole bunch of animals when the world was flooded.

LOT AND HIS DAUGHTERS

@Lot
Relieved to see the back of Sodom (as it were).
Shame my wife became a pillar of salt, but
#shithappens.
1.19pm, 30 March, 0000

@Lot
One of my daughters has got me some wine.
Gonna push the boat out and get wasted tonight.
6.54pm, 2 April, 0000

@Lot
Major league hangover situation going on today,
but my other daughter has also got some wine.
I'm badass.
7.02pm, 3 April, 0000

@Lot
You know when you get so drunk two nights
running that you shag both your daughters? That.
11.48am, 4 April, 0000

Imagine leaving Sodom only to get caught in a
trap of incestuous drunkenness. Funny times.

ASTEROID WIPES OUT DINOSAURS

@DailyExpress
Cave prices doomed as asteroid heads for earth!
See pages 2, 3, 4, 5, 6, 7 – and commemorative
'Oh Crap!' supplement
6.00am, 65,000000 BC

@TRex
@DailyExpress An asteroid? Last week it was
Muslims, before that – chavs, before that –
dangerous dogs. We're, like, whatever!
6.01am, 65,000000 BC

@Asteroid
Hey @Earth, prepare for the ultimate spam...
6.29am, 65,000000 BC

@Earth
Oh shit, where's that 'block' button when you
need it?
6.30am, 65,000000 BC

Dinosaurs are believed to have become extinct
when earth was hit by a huge asteroid
approximately 65 million years ago.

MOSES PARTS THE RED SEA

@Israelites
@Moses Okay, looks like @Pharaoh took your #FF
a tad seriously and is *literally* following us...
5.11 am, 1300 BC

@Pharaoh
I'm coming to get you, @Israelites!
5.14 am, 1300 BC

@Moses
Fear not, @Israelites, watch this... *parts Sea of
Reeds* #swag
7.11 am, 1300 BC

*According to Biblical legend, as the Israelites fled
Egypt they were chased by Pharaoh. When they
arrived at the Red Sea, Moses magically parted
the waters to allow the Israelites safe passage,
and then sent the water crashing over the
Egyptians when they tried to follow.*

THE TEN COMMANDMENTS

@Moses
Totally bored on Mount Sinai. Anyone got any suggestions?
12.34pm, 1301BC

@God
@Moses Have no other gods, no idols, don't blaspheme, keep sabbath, honour your parents, no killing, adultery, theft, lies, or envy.
12.34pm, 1301BC

@Moses
@God OMG – will RT and follow you back!
12.34pm, 1301BC

According to the biblical book of Exodus, God inscribed the Ten Commandments on two stone tablets, and gave them to Moses on Mount Sinai.

THE BUILDING OF THE PYRAMIDS

@PharaohKhufu
I need something built. I want it to be 481ft tall & weigh 5.9million tonnes. Can you recommend someone? A Pole would be nice #pyramidscheme
09.15am, 2540BC

@CairoPractors
@PharaohKhufu See...that's gonna cost ya. We'll need 100,000 men and anticipate it will take around 20 years. Best put the kettle on...
10.12am, 2540BC

@PharaohKhufu
Labourers, eh? I always feel like they're ripping me off but I feel too guilty to argue with the working-classes...
10.13am, 2540BC

The ancient Egyptians built pyramids as tombs for the pharaohs and their queens. The best known, built for the pharaoh Khufu, was the 'Great Pyramid'.

PYTHAGORAS' THEOREM

@Pythagoras
Dudes! In a right-angled triangle the area of the square on hypotenuse is equal to sum of areas of squares of other two sides.
12.01am, November 1, 500BC

@Pythagoras
Or, to put it another way, $a^2 + b^2 = c^2$. Amazing, eh?
12.03am, November 1, 500BC

@IonianTweeter
@Pythagoras Dude, you seriously need to get your leg over.
12.04am, November 1, 500BC

Ancient Greek mathematician Pythagoras could have bested Carol Vorderman when it came to the numbers (but probably not when it came to Rear of the Year contests).

OEDIPUS AND HIS MUM

@Oedipus
#FF @QueenJocasta - now there's a mother I'd love to fuck! #MILF
11.22am, January 2, 492BC

@QueenJocasta
@Oedipus It can be arranged...
11.23am, January 2, 492BC

An Ancient Greek relationship between mother and son, this fling launched a thousand therapists and - so we hear - more than a few lurid internet videos.

GREECE INVENTS DEMOCRACY

@Pericles
Hello peeps! Am thinking of shaking things up, so everybody has a say in how the country is run. Seems fair, innit.
9.30am, 462BC

@GreekWoman
@Pericles *Everybody*?
9.31am, 462BC

@Pericles
@GreekWoman Well, everybody apart from
women, foreigners and slaves. Obvs!
9.32am, 462BC

@GreekWoman
@Pericles This is unfair.
9.33am, 462BC

@Pericles
@GreekWoman Irrelevant. See above.
9.34am, 462BC

@GreekWoman
@Pericles Classy.

*The Ancient Greek aristocrat Pericles is credited
with inventing democracy, in 462BC. However,
not all Greeks were allowed to participate.*

#FAMOUSLASTTWEETS (PART ONE)

@Chrysippus
Just got a donkey drunk and I'm now going to get it to eat figs. This is pure ROFLCOPTER!
8.12pm, April 30, 207BC

The Greek philosopher Chrysippus died the way we all should: laughing at a drunken donkey's attempts to eat figs.

THE TRIAL OF SOCRATES

@Socrates
Got to go to court today for impiety and corrupting the youth. Hoping the News of the Screws don't get on my case about the latter charge.
8.11am, March 22, 399 BC

@Socrates
Got off lightly, all things considered. They just want me to drink this hemlock stuff. BRB.
8.11am, March 22, 399 BC

Socrates died after being sentenced to drink hemlock poison. His epitath: 'the unexamined life is not worth living' would have fitted well into a Tweet.

ALEXANDER THE GREAT

@Greece is now following you
336BC

@Egypt is now following you
332BC

@Arabia is now following you
331BC

@Persia is now following you
330BC

@Mesopotamia is now following you
330BC

@India is now following you
327BC

*In little over a decade the Greek king Alexander
The Great built a massive and formidable empire.
He was undefeated in battle.*

DAVID AND GOLIATH

@Goliath
I've got a little scrap to attend to today. It will be a breeze, you watch...
8.22am, April 5, 1018BC

@Goliath
Ah well. Form is temporary but class lasts forever. Or some such. *Embarrassed*
7.42am, April 5, 1018BC

The first great 'underdog' story saw David the Israelite slay Goliath the Philistine.

JULIUS CAESAR

@JuliusCaesar
Feel like 'extending my empire' – so to speak. @Cleopatra, I'm cumming atcha!
3.40pm, June 4, 53BC

@Cleopatra
@JuliusCaesar Dude, keep it for @NicomedesIV. I'm not interested in being your beard.
3.42pm, June 4, 53BC

'Bloody Hell!..What is a hosepipe ban ?'

@JuliusCaesar
For the last time – I'M NOT GAY! Can someone get me @MaxClifford on the phone?
3.51pm, June 4, 53BC

@PeopleOfRome
Ooooohhh – get her!
3.52pm, June 4, 53BC

@Cassius
Hey, @Brutus: normally @JuliusCaesar is like __/__/__/__ but by the end of today he'll be like _____
6.12am, March 15, 44BC

Roman General Julius Caesar extended the Roman Empire through France, Belgium and beyond. He had an affair with Queen Cleopatra of Egypt but was also rumoured to have enjoyed dalliances with King Nicomedes IV. He was assassinated by a group of senators, spearheaded by Cassius and Brutus.

THE CRUCIFIXION OF JESUS CHRIST

@JesusChrist
Just had supper with 11 pals – stuffed. @Judas
made a pass at me afterwards #awkward
10:02pm 1 April, 33

@JudasIscariot
Thirty pieces of silver – kerching!
10.30pm 1 April, 33

@JesusChrist
Uh oh......
8:40am 3 April, 33

@JesusChrist
I'm back, bitches...
11:43am, 6 April, 33

*Following the Last Supper, Jesus Christ was
betrayed by Judas who identified him with a kiss to
arresting soldiers, who handed him over to Pontius
Pilate. Christ was then crucified and - according to
Christian belief – rose on the third day.*

MOUNT VESUVIUS ERUPTS

@MtVesuvius
Just to put this out there, I'm in a hell of a mood today.
09.01am, August 24, AD79

@PompeiiPeople
@MtVesuvius Well, get her – someone got out of bed the wrong side today!
09.02am, August 24, AD79

@PompeiiPeople
Erm, what the fuck's that plume of smoke in the distance...?
09.03am, August 24, AD79

Mount Vesuvius has erupted several times, most notably in AD79 when it destroyed the Roman cities of Pompeii and Herculaneum. It caught residents unaware, with a 'plume of smoke' on the horizon the first sign of what was afoot.

THE ROMANS INVENT PLUMBING

@Plumbarius
The way we've linked up these aqueducts and
pipes inside people's homes is a bit swag. Soon
we won't have to take a dump outside anymore!
5.12pm AD100

@Plumbarius
We're going into business with this. If you want
your house plumbed up just come to us. We'll give
you a fair price.
5.13pm AD100

@PolishPlumbarius
Whatever price they give you we'll do it for 90
percent less.
5.14pm AD100

@Plumbarius
#FML
5.15pm AD100

*The Roman Empire is credited – blamed? – with
introducing modern plumbing.*

ATTILA THE HUN

@AttilaTheHun
On our way to Rome #roadtrip
4.42pm, March 2, 440

@AttilaTheHun
On our way to Gaul #roadtrip
4.42pm, March 2, 441

@AttilaTheHun
Hmmm, some people got in the way back there.
We had to deal with them. #scourgeofgod
4.42pm, March 2, 441

@AttilaTheHun
On our way to Italy #roadtrip
4.42pm, March 2, 441

@AttilaTheHun
Got married today. Thanks for all your
congratulatory Tweets and DMs. Hang on,
nosebleed...
4.42pm, March 2, 453

Attila The Hun was the leader of the Hunnic
empire and one of the most feared men of his

time. The cause of his death, in 453, is thought to be a colossal nose-bleed on the evening of his wedding day.

THE DOMESDAY BOOK

@WilliamConqueror
#FF Can you follow @DomesdayBook and also Tweet them all your landholdings and resources details? K'bye.
9.00am, March 12, 1085

A detailed survey of land commissioned by William The Conqueror, The Domesday Book now lives at The National Archives, Kew, in South West London.

WE'RE ALL IN THIS TOGETHER (PART ONE)

@KingJohn
Dudes, I'm going to put taxes up a bit. Well, a lot. #We'reAllInThisTogether #Honest
1.18pm, November 2, 1205

War with France created financial issues for England that King John addressed by taxing people like there was no tomorrow.

GENGHIS KHAN

@GenghisKhan
Can't decide whether I fancy a Chinese, a Thai or an Indian. Think I'll have all three. Get the horses, @MrsKhan 6.45pm, April 4, 1211

@GenghisKhan
Might have an Afghan, actually...
4.28pm, October 28, 1213

@GenghisKhan
1) Someone said I have a silly moustache 2) So someone got trampled by a horse 3) And so did 40 million other people
9.12am, August 25, 1277

@GenghisKhan
...some cats and dogs might have got caught in the cross-trample, too. #ShitHappens
9.14am, August 25, 1277

Genghis Khan was one of history's great conquerors. He and his army grabbed an empire including much of Asia and ultimately stretching from the Black Sea to the Pacific. His army was so thorough and heartless it would even destroy the animals of the territories it swept through.

THE MAGNA CARTA

@KingJohn
No freeman shall be taken or imprisoned except by the lawful judgement of his equals or by the law of the land.
9.00 am, June 15, 1215

@KingJohn
To no one will we sell, to no one will we deny or delay right or justice.
9.01 am, June 15, 1215

@KingJohn
PS – Believe that and you'll believe anything. LOL!
9.03 am, June 15, 1215

The Magna Carta was an English charter which reined in the power of the monarchy and subjected it to the rule of law for the first time. Within months King John had reneged on most of the promises contained within it.

THE HUNDRED YEARS WAR

@StopTheWar
Stop The War! #edwardianwar
10.12am, August 1, 1337

@StopTheWar
Stop The War! #bretonwar
4.20pm, October 20, 1341

@StopTheWar
Stop The War! #waroftwopeters
11.11, September 2, 1356

@StopTheWar
Stop The War! #carolinewar
11.49am, May 29, 1369

@StopTheWar
Stop The War! #lancastrianwar
2.02pm, December 20, 1415

@StopTheWar
Oh, why do we even bother!
2.04pm, December 20, 1415

The Hundred Years' War was a series of conflicts and battles between England and France that were fought from 1337 to 1453. A bad time for pacifists.

THE BLACK DEATH

@YeOldePatient
@YeOldeGP Doctor, nearly half the people I know have died. Now I'm starting to feel a bit peaky myself.
9.22am, June 29, 1349

@YeOldeGP
@YeOldePatient Yeah, there's definitely something going around. What are your main symptoms?
9.23am, June 29, 1349

@YeOldePatient

@YeOldeGP I feel like crap and I keep coughing up blood.

9.24am, June 29, 1349

@YeOldeGP

@YeOldePatient Ah, you've obviously just got too much blood. We'll drain some of the excess and you'll be right as rain.

9.25am, June 29, 1349

@YeOldeGP

Okay, that didn't go to plan.

9.27am, June 29, 1349

@YeOldeGP

Feeling a tad rough myself. Going to go for a nap.

2.30pm, June 30, 1349

The Black Death killed up to 45 percent of the British population between 1348 and 1350. Attempts to cure or stop the plague were often primitive and naive.

INVENTION OF THE PRINTING PRESS

@Gutenberg
Invented the printing press today. This is going to democratise publishing. We can now mass-produce written matter.
8.12pm, June 13, 1439

@GermanPrintersUnion
We'd like to announce our first strike. You won't break us.
8.13pm, June 13, 1439

@WilliamCaxton
Just back from Germany. Learned how to mass-print while I was out there. Let's get going!
2.22pm, July 5, 1473

@EnglishPrintersUnion
We'd like to announce our first strike. You won't break us.
2.22pm, July 5, 1473

Johann Gutenberg, a German goldsmith, invented the printing press in 1439. It revolutionised publishing....and industrial relations.

CHRISTOPHER COLUMBUS DISCOVERS
THE NEW WORLD

@ChrisColumb
Trying a #SatNav for the first time today. Going to
let it guide me to the Indies. Bring it on!
6.30am, August 3, 1492

@ChrisColumb
It says we're there now – at last!
5.42pm, October 12, 1492

@ChrisColumb
But the locals are saying we're actually in the
Bahamas. #SatNavFail
5.59pm, October 12, 1492

Perhaps history's finest explorer and navigator,
Christopher Columbus is known as the man who
'discovered' America. He thought the continent he
had arrived at was East Asia – which is why Native
Americans became known as Indians.

THE MONA LISA

@LeonardoDaVinci
OMG – I just met @LisaGherardini! It's true what
they say – she's got a really enigmatic smile.
4.22pm, January 29, 1503

@LeonardosMate
Yeah, right. Pic or it didn't happen!
4.23pm, January 29, 1503

@LeonardoDaVinci
Not lying – I'll Tweet pic it!
4.23pm, January 29, 1503

@LeonardosMate
How's that Tweet pic coming along? I've been
waiting 16 years!
3.55am, February 9, 1519

@LeonardoDaVinci
@LeonardosMate Okay, okay – nearly done!
7.12am, February 9, 1519

*The Mona Lisa is the best known of Leonardo da
Vinci's paintings.*

'I know it's only a dummy run...But I'm telling you there's no wi fi signal in the tomb

HENRY VIII AND HIS SIX WIVES

@Henry_8
Single Ladies (Put a Ring on It) #nowplaying
01.01pm, July 12, 1508

@Henry_8
@ThePope Dude, I'll give you a shout-out if you let
me divorce @CathyAragon
10.12am, November 2, 1530

@ThePope
@Henry_8 No deal.
10.59am, November 2, 1530

@Henry_8
@ThePope You swine – I've done it anyway!
10.59am, May 23, 1533

@ThePope
@Henry_8 *Unfollowed and Blocked*
11.03am, May 23, 1533

@Henry_8
People have been Tweeting me suggesting I could
try and stick with one wife. Lol, it's political
correctness gone mad!
10.23am, June 21, 1533

Henry VIII had six wives. Desperate to produce a male heir, he pleaded with the Pope to grant a divorce from his first wife, Catherine Aragon, but the Pope refused. When Henry divorced her anyway, the Pope excommunicated him.

MICHELANGELO AND THE SISTINE CHAPEL

@Michelangelo
@PopeJuliusII So, I've finally finished that painting you wanted me to do on the wall of the Sistine Chapel. Only took me four years.
5.59pm, January 14, 1512

@PopeJuliusII
@Michelangelo On the *wall*? But I said I wanted it on the *ceiling*!
6.02pm, January 14, 1512

@Michelangelo
@PopeJuliusII What, really? #FML
6.04pm, January 14, 1512

Michelangelo's painting on the roof of the Sistine Chapel, of God giving life to Adam, is one of art's most iconic images.

THE NINE-DAY QUEEN

@JaneGrey
Just got told I've been made Queen. #swag
6.44pm, July 10, 1553

@JaneGrey
Moving into my new posh room at Tower of London. #justcallmeyourmajesty
11.01am, July 11, 1553

@JaneGrey
So, there were some questions in Parliament about my legitimacy as Queen. #amiboverred?
9.11pm, July 15, 1553

@JaneGrey
Can't sleep. Who is this Mary dudess that people keep talking about?
4.12am, July 17, 1553

@JaneGrey

Not so many of my courtiers are about today.
Where's my lunch, for instance?
1.11pm, July 18, 1553

@JaneGrey

No longer Queen. Mary took the gig from me.
Well, that was fun while it lasted.
11.10pm, July 19, 1553

*Lady Jane Grey was Queen of England for just
nine days.*

THE WILLIAM SHAKESPEARE YEARS

@WillShakespeare

2b or not 2b? #thatisthequestion
7.31pm, September 10, 1603

@TwitterBore

@WillShakespeare Let me introduce you to Google
www.google.com
7.32pm, September 10, 1603

@WillShakespeare
Feeling a bit ick today, got a sore throat.
7.31pm, September 10, 1603

@TwitterBore
@WillShakespeare Is it hoarse? A hoarse, a hoarse
- my kingdom for a horse!
7.32pm, September 10, 1603

@WillShakespeare
@TwitterBore Ok, I get it – you're familiar with my
work. But please stop Tweeting. The notifications
keep waking me up and I need to sleep...
7.31pm, September 10, 1603

@TwitterBore
@WillShakespeare ...perchance to dream?
7.32pm, September 10, 1603

@WillShakespeare
@TwitterBore Get thee to a nunnery...*Blocks*
7.31pm, September 10, 1603

*English playwright and poet William Shakespeare
wrote 38 plays, 154 sonnets and several poems.
He is widely considered the greatest ever English
writer and history's finest dramatist.*

#FAMOUSLASTTWEETS (PART TWO)

@FrancisBacon
Quite a blizzard out there tonight. Got me thinking: I wonder if freezing could be a good way of preserving meat?
8.54pm, April 9, 1626

@FrancisBacon
Ok, so I've stuck a chicken out in the snow to see what happens to the meat. If this works out might pitch it at Dragons' Den! #excited
9.22pm, April 9, 1626

Francis Bacon died of pneumonia while studying the effects of freezing.

THE WAR ON WITCHES

@MatthewHopkins
When there's something strange, in your neighbourhood, who you gonna call? Witch hunters!
9.11am, February 2, 1640

@YeOldeTweeter
@MatthewHopkins How do you know if someone is a witch, rather than a non-evil broomstick-bearing old hag?
9.14am, February 2, 1640

@MatthewHopkins
We tie them up and luzz them in a river. If they sink they are innocent, if they float they're guilty. Simples!
9.15am, February 2, 1640

@YeOldeTweeter
@MatthewHopkins Oh
9.17am, February 2, 1640

Witch-hunting in Britain reached its peak in the 1640s, when Puritan Matthew Hopkins held hundreds of trials.

OLIVER CROMWELL

@OllyCrom
Managed to get @KingCharles1st tried and executed today. Back of the sodding net!
11.12pm, January 30, 1649

@OllyCrom

Going to make a few changes now I'm in power:
I'm banning football, theatre-going and pubs. Sod
focus groups, I know how to get popular.
9.31am, December 16, 1653

@OllyCrom

Oh, Happy Christmas by the way!
9.35am, December 16, 1653

@OllyCrom

Got malaria. #FML
5.33am, 3 September 3, 1658

@KingCharles2nd

Going to make a few changes now I'm in power:
let's dig up @OllyCrom's corpse and hang what
remains of it.
9.12am, March 30, 1660

*Oliver Cromwell is one of British history's most
contentious figures. He was a key influence in
getting Charles I executed and then instituted
a puritanical regime. He died of Malaria and
was exhumed for a posthumous execution a year
later. One can only imagine what that must have
looked like.*

ISAAC NEWTON, THE APPLE, AND GRAVITY

@IsaacNewton
Just saw an apple fall from a tree. Got me
thinking: gravity is a universal force.
11.21am, June 2, 1667

@17thCenturyTweeter
OMG! @IsaacNewton just totally got hit on his
head by an apple!
11.22am, June 2, 1667

@IsaacNewton
@17thCenturyTweeter No, I just saw the apple
fall. It didn't hit me on my head.
11.24am, June 2, 1667

@17thCenturyTweeter
@IsaacNewton No. It blates hit you on your head.
Amazeballs. I'm, like, wow!
11.25am, June 2, 1667

@IsaacNewton
@17thCenturyTweeter Whatever.
11.29am, June 2, 1667

A mathematician, physicist and the greatest scientist of his era, Isaac Newton discovered simultaneously that gravity is a universal force and that a mythical legend can spread quickly.

THE GREAT FIRE OF LONDON

@ThomasFarrinor
That nagging doubt you've left the oven on
#IGetThat
10.21pm, September 2, 1666

@SamuelPepys
Fire in London! I'll be live-tweeting it...
11.18pm, September 2, 1666

@FireBrigade
One thing we learned the last few days: the whole 'fighting fire with fire' idea doesn't work for real!
9.14am, September 4 1666

The Great Fire of London broke-out when baker Thomas Farrinor's oven sparked a blaze that went on to destroy over 13,000 homes and make over 65,000 people homeless. The events are documented in the famous diary of Samuel Pepys.

MOZART WRITES HIS FIRST SYMPHONY

@WAMozart
Bored. All my mates are either playing football in
the park or at home with their Playstations. Might
muck about with Dad's piano...
4.21pm, June 1, 1764

*Mozart wrote his first symphony (The Symphony
No. 1 in E flat major) at the age of eight.*

THE DECLARATION OF INDEPENDENCE

@ThomasJefferson
We hold these truths to be self-evident, that all
men are created equal, that they are endowed by
their Creator with certain...
10.11am, July 4, 1776

@ThomasJefferson

...unalienable Rights, that among these are Life, Liberty and the pursuit of Happiness.

10.11am, July 4, 1776

@ThomasDay

@ThomasJefferson Nice words. But what about all those slaves you've got? Are they going to be equal too?

4.22pm, July 4, 1776

The Declaration of Independence formally announced that the American colonies considered themselves as independent states. It attracted admiration but also questions – including from English slavery abolitionist Thomas Day who asked how its author, Thomas Jefferson, squared talk of equality with his own record of holding hundreds of slaves.

THE BRITS STUFF THE FRENCH

@NapoleonBonaparte

Ooh la la...ve have conquered Egypt and now ve vill block ze British trade routes vith India

11.05am, July 1, 1748

@HoratioNelson
Oh no you don't, @NapoleonBonaparte...
2.22pm, August 1, 1748

@NapoleonBonaparte
Okay, zis time we will get the English. Bring on ze Battle of Trafalgar.
6.12am, October 20, 1805

@HoratioNelson
England expects that every man will do his duty.
7.30am, October 20, 1805

@HoratioNelson
French AND Spanish fleets destroyed. None of our ships lost. BOOM!
5.30pm, October 21, 1805

@NapoleonBonaparte
I am still crying – and not just because of ze onions. But we vill get ze English tomorrow at Waterloo.
11.05am, June 17, 1815

@DukeOfWellington
37,000 French troops killed. Battle won.
#MeetYourWaterloo @NapoleonBonaparte!
9.12pm, June 18, 1815

@NapoleonBonaparte
My (short) arse is yours. I surrender.
9.14pm, June 18, 1815

Horatio Nelson and the Duke of Wellington guided Britain to a series of famous victories over France during the 18th and 19th centuries. This culminated in the Battle of Waterloo, after which Napoleon surrendered to the British and was exiled to Saint Helena.

WILLIAM WORDSWORTH

@WilliamWordsworth
So fed up that I haven't got any followers on Twitter. I feel as lonely as a cloud here.
10.13am, April 2, 1804

@WilliamWordsworth
But there is a bliss of solitude. And then my heart with pleasure fills, And dances with the daffodils.
10.14am, April 2, 1804

'How is it Shakespeare didn't get writers' block ?'

@WilliamWordsworth

Oh. Suddenly got a rush of new followers and RTs. Smooth!

10.16am, April 2, 1804

William Wordsworth's poems ushered in the English Romantic Movement. His verses were often influenced by nature and scenery.

THE MADNESS OF KING GEORGE

@KingGeorge

It's great here, isn't it? I love Facebook!

3.12am, April 2, 1814

@KingGeorge

#theawkwardmomentwhen you ruin a dinner party by writhing round on the table, whilst screaming about 12-legged green squirrels

11.59am, October 13, 1815

@KingGeorge
Just did a handstand. A naked handstand. At a funeral. LOL!
3.12am, May 1, 1816

@KingGeorge
#FF No one. Don't follow anyone. Everyone is out to get you. Yipzudooddooo, fgarrrrfeeeelalalalazzzzzzz...
3.12am, February 1, 1817

@KingGeorge
About to eat breakfast: whale vindaloo, couple of pints of petrol and a mattress.
3.12am, July 12, 1818

@KingGeorge
I think my eye sight's going. Fuck a duck – I won't be able to see my Easter eggs tomorrow!
6.22pm, December 24, 1819

@KingGeorge
fvndxnxxf,,ff8z3dx5456,nn559 4-4-44-4-gghOhj;]['@s's''hOhjh
2.12am, December 25, 1819

Having ruled Britain for 59 years, King George III suffered from dementia and blindness in the last years of his life. He died in 1820 at Windsor Castle.

THE LAUNCH OF THE *GUARDIAN* NEWSPAPER

@Grauniad
Tody we luanch the newspapre: a front page splash about a Nicaraguan poet, a lentil recipe, social worker job ads and bisexual horoscopes.
6.05am, May 5, 1821

@Grauniad
Our slogan will be: Comment is free, but facts are scared
6.06am, May 5, 1821

@GrauniadReader
@Grauniad Comrades, I noticed quite a few errors in your paper today
11.02pm, May 5, 1821

@Grauniad
You're joking, right? LOAM!
11.42pm, May 5, 1821

The Guardian *newspaper – first called the* Manchester Guardian *– was launched in 1821.*

THE FIRST POSTAGE STAMP

@Correspondent
So excited about the Penny Black postage stamp that got launched today. Am queuing at the post office to send my first letter.
9.31am, May 1, 1840

@Correspondent
Still queuing.
9.31am, May 1, 1940

@Correspondent
Actually still queuing.
9.31am, May 1, 1980

@Correspondent
Fuck it – I'll Tweet them instead.
9.31am, July 15, 2006

The world's first official adhesive postage stamp, the Penny Black, was first issued in Britain in

1840. The English love of queuing was about to get sorely tested.

THE COMMUNIST MANIFESTO

@KarlMarx
The history of all hitherto existing society is the history of class struggle.
10.05am, February 21, 1848

@FriedrichEngels
Dude, I'm totally up for this #communism thing.
What could possibly go wrong?
10.06am, February 21, 1848

@JosephStalin
@KarlMarx @FriedrichEngels Hello...
10.06am, December 18, 1879

The Communist Manifesto, written by Karl Marx and Friedrich Engels, was published in 1848. It lay the foundation of the communist movement. Joseph Stalin became the supreme ruler of the Soviet Union, causing the suffering and deaths of tens of millions of people.

INVENTION OF MORSE CODE AND TELEGRAPHY

@SamuelMorse
Twitter is all very well but I've just developed a
much better way of communicating. Just use dots,
dashes, dits and dahs. #MorseCode
11.06pm, June 15, 1835

@SamuelMorse
It's going to be amazing! What do you think:
awesome or what?
11.09pm, June 15, 1835

@SamuelMorse
Anyone?
11.22pm, June 15, 1835

@SamuelMorse
Okay, how about this one. *Stop* I'll call it the
telegraph. *Stop* What do you think of it? *Stop*
Better than Twitter, innit? *Stop*
4.12pm, May 24 1844

@SamuelMorse
Why do I even bother?
4.14pm, May 24 1844

Morse code and telegraphy, both invented by Samuel Morse, revolutionised communications and were, in a sense, forerunners of Twitter.

THE CHARGE OF THE LIGHT BRIGADE

@LordRaglan
@LordLucan Advance rapidly to the front and try to prevent the enemy carrying away the guns
11.20am, October 24, 1848

@LordLucan
What does that even mean? Shall I check? Nah, can't be arsed. Oi, @CavalryMen: attack, attack attack!
11.20am, October 24, 1848

@LordTennyson
Into the Valley of Death/Rode the six hundred... Cannon to the right of them/Cannon to the left of them...
9.12pm, October 24, 1848

A misunderstood order during the Crimean War sent over 600 British cavalrymen running into heavy Russian gunfire. Up to 200 died and the event was immortalised in a poem from Lord Tennyson.

THE CALIFORNIAN GOLD RUSH...

@JWMarshall
Score! Just struck gold in San Francisco! Gonna party hard tonight. RT if you wanna join me!
6.20pm, January 24, 1849
[ReTweeted by @GoldHunter and 29,999 others.]

...AND AMERICA ENTERS THE OIL INDUSTRY

@EdwinDrake
To everyone who called me 'crazy': I just struck oil. So we Americans are now in the oil trade. What could possibly go wrong?
8.12pm, August 28, 1859

The discoveries of huge reserves of gold and oil in America caused huge excitement in the 19th century.

THE DEATH OF JOHN SEDGWICK

@JohnSedgwick
What? Men dodging this way for single bullets? I am ashamed of you. They couldn't hit an elephant at this distance...
11.19am, May 9, 1864

Union Army General John Sedgwick died during the Battle of Spotsylvania Court House, just seconds after chastising his troops.

THE ASSASSINATION OF ABRAHAM LINCOLN

@AbrahamLincoln
Such a relief that the whole #Confederacy thing is over. For a while back there I was worried it was going to get even nastier.
11.11pm, April 9, 1865

@AbrahamLincoln
Off to the theatre tonight. I've heard there are some really funny moments in the play. Got a private box. #swag
5.12pm April 14, 1865

@AbrahamLincoln
LOL! This play is really funn
8.23pm April 14, 1865

The presidency of Abraham Lincoln, the 16th president of the United States, was dominated by the American Civil War. Less than a week after the Confederate general Robert E Lee surrendered, Lincoln was assassinated during a performance at Ford's Theatre in Washington DC. The assassin waited until the auditorium was filled with laughter to strike.

THE INVENTION OF THE TELEPHONE

@GrahamBell
Just been awarded a patent for a new product called the telephone. We can use them to Tweet people.
4.45pm, March 2, 1876

@GrahamBell
We'll not only be able to Tweet on them – we'll be able to speak to people using our actual voices!
4.46pm, March 2, 1876

@Graham's_mother_in_law
@GrahamBell This is great news, now we can speak every day! #justsaying
4.46pm, March 2, 1876

@GrahamBell
Is it possible to un-invent something? #justasking
4.47pm, March 2, 1876

@Graham's_mother_in_law
@GrahamBell Awww, come on – it's good to talk!
4.48pm, March 2, 1876

Alexander Graham Bell is credited with the invention of the telephone. Sometimes it seems like a good idea, sometimes less so.

THE ANGLO-ZANZIBAR WAR

@TheUK
@Zanzibar Oi you – it's war!
9.00am, 27 August, 1896

@19thCenturyTweeter
Fight! Fight! Fight! *Grabs popcorn*
9.01am, 27 August, 1896

@Zanzibar
@TheUK Okay, you win!
9.38am, 27 August, 1896

@19thCenturyTweeter
Oh, borrrr-rring!!! *Sighs*
9.41am, 27 August, 1896

The war between the United Kingdom and the Zanzibar Sultanate was the shortest of history, lasting – by most estimates – a mere 38 minutes.

VICTORIAN ENGLAND

@VictorianToddler
Can't wait till I grow up. When I'm four I'll start working in the mine and by the time I'm eight I want to be a chimney sweep. #ambitions
4.12pm, June 21, 1842

@VictorianTeenager
Anyone looking for business? I'll give you a good time in return for a Twitter shout-out.
11.34pm, August 30, 1851

@VictorianAdult

Just off to work: an 18-hour day of needlework.
The pay? Practically nowt.

6.12am, February 10, 1872

@QueenVic

The important thing is not what they think of me,
but what I think of them.

4.22pm, November 22, 1897

The Victorian era was a time of child labour,
rampant prostitution and widespread poverty.

THE INVENTION OF AIR TRAVEL

@OrvilleWright

Me and @WilburWright have just flown an
airplane for the first time! #swag

3.12am, December 17, 1903

@WilburWright

I know, right? This is a game-changer for travel:
no more frustrating delays or hanging round for
hours!

3.12am, December 17, 1903

@AirHostess
The flight is delayed. Did you pack those bags
yourself? Can you turn your phone off & put your
head-rest up please? Have some plastic food.
3.13am, December 17, 1903

@OrvilleWright
Sheesh. Okay, nobody said it was perfect. But
what could possibly go wrong?
3.12am, December 17, 1903

@MohamedAtta
We have some planes. Stay where you are and you
won't get hurt.
8.52am, September 11, 2011

*The Wright brothers, a pair of bike mechanics
from Ohio, invented air travel when they flew the
first aeroplane in 1903. Commercial and then
passenger travel soon took off.*

'Mr Bell: instead of "amazeballs" could you just use "hello".'

ALBERT EINSTEIN

@AlbertEinstein
OMG, I just worked out that E totally equals mc²!
#Simples
4.19pm, June 1, 1905

@AlbertEinstein
Sorry I've not Tweeted for a while. But I've realised that time and space are relative. Not fixed. Do you get me? #theoryofrelativity
4.19am, January 30, 1916

The eminent scientist and originator of the theory of relativity Albert Einstein would have been an informative, if occasionally baffling, Tweeter.

#FAMOUSLASTTWEETS (PART THREE)

@CaptLawrenceOates
On an Antarctic mission. It's cold as fuck here. I am just going outside. I won't BRB – I actually may be some time.
9.12am, March 16, 1912

Antarctic explorer Captain Oates' last words have become iconic.

THE SINKING OF THE TITANIC

@TitanicSkipper
Pulling out of Southampton. Can't wait for the Big Apple. Off to arrange the deck-chairs.
10:23am, 10 April, 1912

@TitanicSkipper
Iceberg ahead, but it's all good – we're #practicallyunsinkable
11:39pm, 14 April, 1912

Heralded as 'practically unsinkable' the Titanic ocean liner struck an iceberg at 11.40pm on 14 April, 1912 during her voyage from Southampton to New York. Within two hours and 40 minutes she had sunk deep into the freezing Atlantic waters. Less than a third of those on board survived.

THE BRITISH EMPIRE

@BritEmpire
We've now got 400million followers. Back of the net!
10.01am, June 1, 1913

At its height the British Empire ruled 400 million people.

WORLD WAR ONE

@Austria
@Serbia Are you looking at me?
9.31pm June 28, 1914

@Germany
@Russia Did you spill my pint?
August 1914

@Germany
@France What you staring at?
August 1914

@Belgium
@Germany Nah, what are YOU staring at?
August 1914

@Britain
@Germany Come and 'ave a go if you think you're
'ard enough!
August 1914

@France
@Austria Do you want some?
August 1914

@Britain
@Austria Fuck them – are you staring at my bird?
August 1914

@Germany
@USA Come on then – we'll have you all!
August 1914

@Britain
@Germany Re your humiliating defeat, the best
thing is just to move on. Don't dwell on it
whatever you do!
11:00am, November 11, 1918

World War One left Germany feeling humiliated...

THE RISE OF ADOLF HITLER

@AdolfHitler
Just got up and realised the milk in the fridge has gone off. Going to have to walk to the shops. Overwhelmed by the injustice of this.
8.24am, 12 January, 1924

@AdolfHitler
Okay, had my tea. On my way to work now but I was running late because of the milk saga. Missed the bus.
8.59am, 12 January, 1924

@AdolfHitler
Got the next bus but it's crowded. Going to have to stand the whole way! I need a hash-tag for all this. How about #mystruggle?
9.22am, 12 January, 1924

@AdolfHitler
For fuck's sake. The woman at the office canteen is off today. I had to cut my sandwich myself! #mystruggle
2.01pm, 12 January, 1924

@AdolfHitler

Sorry I haven't Tweeted for a few days. Dropped my iPhone down the loo. Proves my point though, about #mystruggle. Can we get it trending?
9.12am, 14 January, 1924

Adolf Hitler's memoir, Mein Kampf – *or My Struggle – was published in the mid-1920s. Historians have found that his early years were notable for their lack of struggle and abundance of comfort.*

THE BIRTH OF THE BBC

@BBC

Coming up: Eldorado, carrots that look like cocks on That's Life, @Wossy interviews @RickyGervais, and Moira Stewart gets a hairdo.
9.00am, 12 March, 1929

The British Broadcasting Corporation began transmission in 1929.

WINSTON CHURCHILL V THE LADIES

@LadyAstor
@WinstonChurchill If you were my husband, I'd
poison your tea.
8.55pm, February 2, 1937

@WinstonChurchill
@LadyAstor Madam, if you were my wife, I'd
drink it.
8.56pm, February 2, 1937

@BessieBraddock
@WinstonChurchill You're drunk!
9.01pm, March 30, 1937

@WinstonChurchill
@BessieBraddock Yes, madam, I am drunk.
But in the morning I will be sober and you will still
be ugly.
9.02pm, March 30, 1937

@WinstonChurchill
LOL. Am a bit wasted, TBH. Gonna get myself a
doner kebab.
9.09pm, March 30, 1937

One of Britain's wittiest men, Winston Churchill had a pithy response for most attempts at putdowns. He'd have been a majestic Tweeter.

THE HINDENBURG DISASTER

@MaxPruss
Wondering if I told everyone about the no-smoking rule...
4.01pm, May 6, 1937

The Hindenburg, a German passenger airship, was destroyed by fire in 1937.

NEVILLE CHAMBERLAIN

@NevilleSayNeville
Just landed at #Heathrow after my meeting with @AdolfHitler I've secured peace for our time – he gave me a piece of paper to prove it!
3.48pm, 30 September, 1938

@AdolfHitler

Had a LMAO meeting with @NevilleSayNeville –
what a guy. I'm having an early night, as we're
marching into the Sudetenland tomorrow.
8.02pm, 30 September, 1938

@AdolfHitler

Probably won't return any #FFs this week, cos
we're invading Bohemia and Slovakia.
#pieceofpapermyarse
6.01am, 15 March, 1939

@NevilleSayNeville

The awkward moment when @AdolfHitler invades
Poland. Beginning to think the piece of paper was
a ploy. I'm, like, totally declaring #war.
2.01 pm, 1 September, 1939

*When Neville Chamberlain signed the Munich
Agreement with Germany in 1938, he claimed he
had secured 'peace for our time'. However,
Germany continued to invade foreign lands,
leaving both the Agreement and Chamberlain's
credibility in tatters.*

PEARL HARBOUR

@EmperorHirohito
118 ships and vessels sunk or damaged, 164 aircraft destroyed, 2,400 Yanks killed. Mission accomplished.
10.02am, December 7, 1941

@PresidentRoosevelt
This is a day that will live in infamy. We declare war on Japan.
11.11am, December 8, 1941

@EmperorHirohito
People keep asking if I'm worried about the Yanks declaring war on us. Worried? Oh pur-lease! I mean, what's the worst that could happen?
12.40pm, December 8, 1941

When Japan launched an unexpected attack on the naval base at Pearl Harbor in Hawaii, it stunned America. The attack led directly to American entry into World War Two.

THE INVENTION OF THE NUCLEAR BOMB

@JROppenheimer
Bit bored so thought I'd see what happens if you
assemble a mass of fissile material into a
supercritical mass. Quite a lot, it turns out.
5.31am, July 6, 1945

@JROppenheimer
I am become death. The destroyer of worlds.
5.32am, July 6, 1945

@KennethBainbridge
@JROppenheimer Yup, now we are all sons of
bitches.
5.33am, July 6, 1945

*J Robert Oppenheimer was the head of the
Manhattan Project: the development programme
that produced the first nuclear bomb. On
witnessing the successful detonation of the
world's first nuclear bomb, he quoted a passage
from* The Bhagavad Gita. *Test director Kenneth
Bainbridge's reported words were just as apt.*

HIROSHIMA AND NAGASAKI

@MayorOfHiroshima
What the fuck was that bang? #famouslasttweets
8.16am, August 6, 1945

@HarrySTruman
@MayorOfHiroshima That was 'Little Boy' named
after @President Roosevelt
8.16am, August 6, 1945

@PresidentRoosevelt
@HarrySTruman Scuse me! You're not exactly a
horse yourself from what I've heard.
8.17am, August 6, 1945

@MayorOfNagasaki
What the fuck was that bang? #famouslasttweets
11.01am, August 9, 1945

@HarrySTruman
@MayorOfNagasaki That was 'TheFatMan', named
after @WinstonChurchill.
8.16am, August 9, 1945

@WinstonChurchill

@HarrySTruman @PresidentRoosevelt Better a fat man than a little boy, no?
8.17am, August 9, 1945

@StephenFry

@HarrySTruman @MayorOfHiroshima @MayorOfNagasaki Oh, must you all be so beastly to each other? I'm leaving Twitter!
8.18am, August 9, 1945

America dropped two atomic bombs on Japan in August 1945. First, the 'Little Boy' bomb was dropped on Hiroshima, killing over 100,000 people. Three days later America dropped the 'Fat Man' bomb on Nagasaki, killing over 74,000 people.

THE COLD WAR

@TheUSofA

So we've got nuclear bombs.
10.00am, August 10, 1945

@TheSoviets
So have we.
11.02pm, August 29, 1949

@TheUSofA
We had them first.
0.01am, January 1, 1950

@TheSoviets
What's your point?
0.01am, January 1, 1960

@TheUSofA
Nothing – just saying.
0.01am, January 1, 1970

@TheSoviets
Whatever
0.01am, January 1, 1980

@TheUSofA
Tsssk
0.01am, January 1, 1989

Between the end of World War Two and the
collapse of the Soviet Union in the 1990s,
international relations were defined by the tense
nuclear stand-off between the East and West.

'Some gobbledegook from Titanic...*LOL*...then two hours later, *OMG*.'

PRINCE CHARLES IS BORN

@PrincePhilip
Welcome to the world – and Twitter –
@PrinceCharles. So proud. I'd like him to have the
things I wasn't able to have.
11.01pm, 14 November, 1948

@PrincePhilip
India, for instance.
11.03pm, 14 November, 1948

*By the time Prince Charles was born the British
Empire was a thing of the past.*

THE RISE OF FEMINISM

@SimonedeBeauvoir
I'm publishing a book today about the bad
treatment of women throughout history. It's
called *The Second Sex*.
9.29am, June 1, 1949

@MaleTweeter
Giggle, she said 'sex'! Pffffftttttt...
9.31am, June 1, 1949

@GermaineGreer
I'm publishing a book about feminism. It's called
The Female Eunuch.
9.31am, May 2, 1970

@MaleTweeter
She said 'eunuch'. Hahahahaha!
9.32am, May 2, 1970

@SimonedeBeauvoir
@GermaineGreer Can you believe how immature
men are?
10.55am, May 2, 1970

@MichaelWinner
Calm down, dear, it's just Twitter.
10.57am, May 2, 1970

The rise of feminism has had many triumphs.
Some parts of the human race are beyond its
reach.

GEORGE ORWELL PUBLISHES
NINETEEN EIGHTY FOUR

@GeorgeOrwell
In the future, people will be able to monitor our
every move, and the cult of personality will rule.
#BigBrother
9.30am, June 8, 1949

@Twitter
@GeorgeOrwell Interesting idea that, there could
be a business in it...
9.31am, June 8, 1949

@DavinaMcCall
#BigBrother will get back to you...
9.59pm, July 18, 2000

*George Orwell's story of a dystopian future in his
novel Nineteen Eighty Four has fascinated readers
since the book was published in the 1940s.
Debate over the extent that his vision has or will
come true makes his book a true benchmark.*

#FAMOUSLASTTWEETS (PART FOUR)

@IvanTheTerrible
Playing chess with @BogdanBelsky – I'm so
gonna win!
6.22pm, March 28, 1954

@BodganBelsky
@IvanTheTerrible Lol, looks like I won this one.
6.23pm, March 28, 1954

*Ivan the Terrible died of a stroke whilst playing
chess.*

JFK AND MARILYN MONROE

@MarilynMonroe
#FF @JFK Happy birthday, Mr President.
11.32am, May 18, 1962

DM from @JKF to @MarilynMonroe
Ssssh, I told you – not on Twitter.
11.33am, May 18, 1962

In one of her final public appearances, Marilyn Monroe sang to President John F Kennedy for his 45th birthday. The two are believed to have had an affair.

THE CUBAN MISSILE CRISIS

@JFK
Bit of a drama going down with the Commies over some missiles in Cuba. #touchingcloth
11.12am, October 14, 1962

@Khrushchev
@JFK That'll learn you for putting missiles in Turkey!
11.13am, October 14, 1962

@JFK
Sheesh, this is worse than the Vienna Summit and the Bay of Pigs combined
11.21am, October 14, 1962

@Khrushchev
@JFK LOL!
11.23am, October 14, 1962

@JFK
Reached agreement with the Commies over Cuba.
Glad that's all sorted. Life doesn't get worse.
12.29pm, October 28, 1962

*In 1962, Russian Premier Nikita Khrushchev
installed nuclear weapons in Cuba to defend it
from US invasion. After the missiles were spotted
by a US spy plane, the world teetered on the brink
of nuclear war for a week.*

THE ASSASSINATION OF JFK

@JFK
Touched down in Dallas and now driving through
this beautiful city. Life doesn't get any better.
12.29pm, November 22, 1963

@LeeHarveyO
Ich bin ein bad killer!
12.31pm, November 22, 1963

*President John F Kennedy was assassinated in
Dallas in 1963. The killer was Lee Harvey Oswald.*

MARTIN LUTHER KING'S SPEECH

@MartinLKing
Morning all. I had an amazing dream last night.
There were these 4 kids, some valleys &
mountains. I think it could change the world.
8.02am, August 28, 1963
[Retweeted by @DC_Dude and 249,999 others]

*Martin Luther King delivered his legendary 'I have
a dream' speech on the steps of the Lincoln
Memorial in Washington on 28 August, 1963.*

THE 'WISDOM' OF PRINCE PHILIP

@PrincePhilip
Sorry I haven't tweeted for a while. Am looking
forward to using it to express my view of the
world!
7.57pm, March 1, 1966

@PrincePhilip
British women can't cook!
7.58pm, March 1, 1966

@PrincePhilip
What's everyone's problem with this recession?
Everybody was saying we must have more leisure.
Now they are complaining they are unemployed.
5.12pm, May 21, 1981

@PrincePhilip
Gosh, there are some sensitive little flowers on
Twitter, aren't there?
5.14pm, May 21, 1981

@PrincePhilip
The trouble with @PrincessAnne is that if it
doesn't fart or eat hay then she isn't interested.
4.18am, June 23, 1988

@PrincePhilip
I wonder how Scottish driving instructors keep
the natives off the booze long enough to pass
the test...
2.22pm, September 22, 1995

@PrincePhilip
Oops! Just got a load more un-follows!
2.23pm, September 22, 1995

@PrincePhilip

Saw a fuse box earlier. It was a right mess. Looked as though it had been put in by an Indian.

3.39am, October 12, 2002

@PrincePhilip

Met some Aborigines today. Asked if they still throw spears at one another.

8.12pm, November 1, 2002

@PrincePhilip

There's a lot of orphanages in Romania – they must breed them.

4.44pm, July 1, 2010

@QueenLiz2

@PrincePhilip One thinks we need a chat about you and Twitter...

Prince Philip has distinguished himself as one of Britain's most outspoken figures with colourful views and observations throughout his life.

ENGLAND WINS THE WORLD CUP

@ThreeLionArmy
Running onto the pitch at Wembley. We think it's all over.
5.13pm, July 30, 1966

@KennethWolstenholme
It is now!
5.14pm, July 30, 1966

Kenneth Wolstenholme's commentary of England's 1966 World Cup Final victory over Germany has become legendary.

THE SIX DAY WAR

@Syria
Pssst – ourselves, @Egypt, @Iraq and @Jordan have got a little surprise lined-up for the Jews!
8:14am, June 5, 1967

@TheJews

Pssst – we've got a little surprise lined-up ourselves...

8:15am, June 5, 1967

In June 1967, the armies of several Arab states prepared to attack the Jewish state of Israel. Egyptian state radio vowed to 'Wipe Israel off the map'. Israel launched a pre-emptive strike and defeated all five armies in just six days.

THE SUMMER OF LOVE

@TheFlowerChildren

They say if you Tweeted during the summer of love then you weren't there...

7.12pm, July 5, 1967

During the summer of 1967 hundreds of thousands of hippies gathered in American cities including San Francisco, New York, Los Angeles, and across Europe. These get-togethers became melting pots of drugs, sex and creative expression.

MAN ON THE MOON

@NeilArmstrong
Ha – me and @BuzzAldrin are chilling on the
moon! One small step for man, one giant leap for
mankind. #wishihadmygolfclubs
02.56, July 21, 1969

@TheSoviets
Pics or it didn't happen...
09:32am, July 22, 1969

*American Neil Armstrong has become the first
man to walk on the Moon on July 22, 1969. He
was joined by his colleague Edwin 'Buzz' Aldrin.
The Soviet Union – and conspiracy theorists to
this day – contest whether American astronauts
ever achieved this feat.*

ANDY WARHOL

@AndyWarhol
In the future everybody will be world famous for
140 characters or fewer.
6.55pm, September 1, 1969

Andy Warhol, artist, film-maker and author, predicted that in the future everybody would be famous for 15 minutes. Thanks to Twitter, he was almost right.

PUNK ROCK

@PunkRockSkool
Learn a chord, learn another chord, learn a third chord – now go and form a band.
10.21pm, June 2, 1976

@SteveJones
@BillGrundy You dirty fucker!
6.58pm, December 1, 1976

@BillGrundy
@SteveJones What a clever boy!
6.58pm, December 1, 1976

@SteveJones
@BillGrundy What a fucking rotter!
6.59pm, December 1, 1976

@JohnnyRotten
#FF @QueenLiz2 – the fascist regime, she made you a moron...
2.01pm, March 10, 1977

@QueenLiz2
@JohnnyRotten Takes one to know one, one has always thought...
2.01pm, March 10, 1977

@SidVicious
Feels good to be out on bail. I'm ready to party...
4.48pm, February 1, 1979

Punk Rock, which exploded in 1976, was spearheaded in Britain by The Sex Pistols. They shocked the nation by swearing at Bill Grundy on tea-time television, and producing their own anti-Jubilee song. Bassist Sid Vicious later died of a heroin overdose while out on bail for the murder of his former girlfriend, Nancy Spungen.

'And if I do this I get far better reception.'

ELVIS PRESLEY DIES

@TheKing
Just popping to the bathroom. BRB.
3.30pm, August 16, 1977

@ElvisLackey
The King is dead. (I wouldn't go in there for a bit.)
4.21pm, August 16, 1977

*Elvis Presley died in the toilet of his mansion in
Memphis on 16 August 1977. He was 42.*

RUSSIANS IN AFGHANISTAN

@Mujahideen
@TheCIA Hey, thanks for all the money and support
as we fight to kick the Soviets out of Afghanistan
4.55am, August 1, 1979

@TheCIA
@Mujahideen Don't even mention it. You're very
welcome.
8.44am, August 1, 1979

@Mujahideen
@TheCIA Homies forever?
8.54am, August 1, 1979

@TheCIA
@Mujahideen We'll get back to you on that.
8.56am, August 1, 1979

In 1979, the CIA began to fund and support the Afghan Mujahideen rebels in their bid to get the Soviet army out of Afghanistan. One beneficiary of this funding and support was a young man called Osama Bin Laden.

JOHN LENNON MURDERED

@JohnLennon
Imagine all the people, living in harmony...
22.59pm, December 08, 1980

@MarkChapman
Yeah, imagine that...
23.01pm, December 08, 1980

@JohnLennon
We're bigger than...JESUS!
23.01pm, December 08, 1980

@PaulMacca
Just heard the sad news about @JohnLennon. Talk about a hard day's night! *Must remember to reverse song-writing credits*
5.02am, December 09, 1980

John Lennon was shot dead outside his New York apartment by gunman Mark Chapman in December 1980.

CHARLES AND DIANA MARRY

@LadyDi
@PrinceCharles Oh, Chazza, I totally <3 you!
11:20am, July 29, 1981

@PrinceCharles
Whatever <3 means.
11.21am, July 29, 1981

DM from @CamillaParkerBowles
@PrinceCharles Dinner?
11.22am, July 29, 1981

A crowd of 600,000 people lined the streets of London to cheer as Prince Charles and Lady Diana Spencer arrived at St Paul's Cathedral to marry. As their marriage subsequently fell apart, Diana complained about Charles's continued affections with Camilla Parker-Bowles. They divorced in August 1996.

MICHAEL JACKSON

@MichaelJackson
Yoo-hoo – what an eventful night I just had! Feeling drained but inspired. Headed to the studio to lay-down a new track.
08.01am, June 09, 1982

@MichaelJackson
Nailed the new song – it's called P.Y.T. (Pretty Young Thing).
12.52pm, June 09, 1982

@Bubbles
@MichaelJackson Pretty young thing? Interesting title – what inspired that?
4.43pm, June 09, 1982

@MichaelJackson
@Bubbles *Blushes*
5.12pm, June 09, 1982

@MichaelJackson
@MacaulayCulkin I just watched your film – *Home Alone*. Three times in a row. You're enchanting. Follow me back?
3.01am, November 16, 1990

@MacaulayCulkin
@MichaelJackson Sure – what's the worst that can happen?
7.57am, November 16, 1990

@Bubbles
@MichaelJackson Oh, you're bad...
8.11am, November 16, 1990

@MichaelJackson
@Bubbles (Really, Really Bad!)
8.12am, November 16, 1990

@MichaelJackson

By the way, has anyone seen my nose? I can't remember when I last had it.
2.09am, June 12, 1994

During an eventful life, Michael Jackson sold many millions of records and played sell-out tours in huge stadiums. Allegations of child abuse, his ever-changing facial appearance and a host of eccentricities meant the King of Pop became better known as Wacko Jacko.

RONALD REAGAN

@RonaldReagan

My fellow Americans, I'm pleased to tell you that I've signed legislation that will outlaw Russia forever. We begin bombing in five minutes.
10.01am, August 11, 1984

@WhiteHouseStaff

Just FYI, @KonstantinChernenko, the President was only joking.
10.02am, August 11, 1984

@KonstantinChernenko
@WhiteHouseStaff Very droll, I'm sure.
10.02am, August 11, 1984

DM from @TheIronLady
To @RonaldReagan: Well, who's been a naughty
boy, then?
10.03am, August 11, 1984

DM from @RonaldReagan
To @TheIronLady: Sorry, Ma'am, can you remind
me who you are? Hello? Is that you Nancy?
11.31am, August 11, 1984

*Ronald Reagan, President of the United States
between 1981 and 1989, had a colourful career
with public gaffes, an assassination attempt and
a close relationship with Margaret Thatcher.*

LIVE AID

@MichaelBuerk
Millions of people are starving Ethiopia.
Somebody needs to do something about this.
9.01pm, October 23, 1984

@BobGeldof

@MichaelBuerk I'll put on a fundraising rock concert. Hopefully the egos won't take over. #LiveAid

9.10pm, October 23, 1984

@PhilCollins

I'm going to fly between at England and America so I can perform at both Live Aid gigs – it's all about me!

3.39pm, July 13, 1985

@NoelEdmonds

Hang on, I'll helicopter you to the airport – it's all about me!

3.40pm, July 13, 1985

@FreddieMercury

@PhilCollins @NoelEdmonds Erm, hello? I think you'll find it's all about meeeee!

7.03pm, July 13, 1985

@BobGeldof

No, it's about the people dying *now*. Don't go to the pub, stay in and give us your money. FUCK THE ADDRESS!

7.45pm, July 13, 1985

After Michael Buerk's shocking BBC news report about the Ethiopian famine, rock star Bob Geldof organised dual fundraising concerts in London and New York. A global audience of 1.9 billion people tuned in, and around £50million was raised for famine relief.

THE CHERNOBYL DISASTER

@ChernobylWorker
Bad day at the office today. Long story short: one the nuclear reactors blew-up. Far from ideal.
1.24am, April 16, 1986

@Pravda
@ChernobylWorker Ve have vays of making you delete your Tweets...
1.25am, April 16, 1986

@ChernobylWorker
Gulp
1.26am, April 16, 1986

@SwedishGovernment
@SovietUnion Erm, dudes, has some shit

happened? We're getting, like, radioactive fallout from over your way.
8.17am, April 18, 1986

@SovietUnion
Nope, nothing to see here. @Gorbachev just had a bit of a dodgy curry...
8.17am, April 18, 1986

@ThePentagon
@SovietUnion Don't you think you should warn people about this 'nuclear vindaloo'?
10.12am, April 19, 1986

@SovietUnion
@ThePentagon No, there are weddings & parades coming up – we don't want to put a dampener on them. Calm down, dear, it's only a reactor!
10.13am, April 18, 1986

Following an explosion at the Chernobyl nuclear plant in 1986, radiation hundreds of times greater than the fallout from the Hiroshima and Nagasaki bombs was sent into the atmosphere. As the radiation spread, Soviet authorities were very slow to admit what had happened. Meanwhile, residents of nearby neighbourhoods held open-air weddings and May Day parades, unaware of the radiation in the air. Estimates of how many ultimately died as a result of the disaster vary, with some running into the hundreds of thousands.

MADONNA

@Madonna
True, a lot of my videos are on the steamy side but I make no apology for making the most of it while I'm young.
10.12am, July 25, 1987

@Madonna
I mean – it would be a bit sad if I was still behaving like this when I hit my 50s!
10.13am, July 25, 1987

Madonna's raunchy pop videos provoked simultaneous outrage and delight throughout the 1980s. She hasn't let it lie since.

THE FALL OF THE IRON CURTAIN

@BerlinMayor
Feeling so moved that the Berlin Wall has come down. We need an event to celebrate our new found freedom and the end of tyranny. Any ideas?
11.13pm, November 9, 1989

@DavidHasselhoff
@BerlinMayor I could perform a New Year concert on the remains of the Wall?
11.17pm, November 9, 1989

@BerlinMayor
Actually, is it too late to put the Wall back up?
11.19pm, November 9, 1989

When the Wall that had kept east and west Berlin apart for three decades finally came down, who would have thought that Knight Rider and Baywatch star David Hasselhoff would headline the celebratory concert?

THE RELEASE OF NELSON MANDELA

@NelsonMandela
@WinnieMandela Did you tape #CoronationStreet
while I was away? I expect that @HildaOgden is
still an interfering old bat!
4.14pm, February 11, 1990

@WinnieMandela
@NelsonMandela Er, we can come to that – we've
got a lot to talk about.
4.15pm, February 11, 1990

@NelsonMandela
@WinnieMandela Answer the question: did you
tape Corrie – yes, or no?
4.15pm, February 11, 1990

@WinnieMandela
@NelsonMandela No. I've been a bit busy
kidnapping and assaulting people.
4.15pm, February 11, 1990

@NelsonMandela
@WinnieMandela BIYYYYYAAATCH! I'm divorcing
you!
4.15pm, February 11, 1990

Leading anti-apartheid Nelson Mandela was released from prison in South Africa after 27 years in February 1990. Four years later he was elected President.

GAZZA'S TEARS

@Gazza
Now @GaryLineker has equalised we cannae affords any more slips, leeke.
9.47pm, July 4, 1990

@Gazza
Take that, @ThomasBerthold!
9.48pm, July 4, 1990

@TheRef
@Gazza You're booked, son!
9.49pm, July 4, 1990

@Gazza
Fuck, I'm out of the final now. A booo hooo hooo hooo, leeke!
9.50pm, July 4, 1990

'Houston...the commander took his glove off to microblog...'

@GaryLineker
@BobbyRobson Have a word with him! *Pulls strange expression and tries not to shit himself*
9.50pm, July 4, 1990

@RaoulMoat
Gutted for @Gazza, I just want to take him a can of lager, some chicken, a mobile phone and something to keep warm...
9.55pm, July 4, 1990

@ChrisWaddle
@Gazza @GaryLineker @BobbyRobson @RaoulMoat Divvun worry, we'll cock-up the penalties anyway, leeke.
9.56pm, July 4, 1990
[Retweeted by @StuartPearce]

Paul 'Gazza' Gascoigne's tears after a yellow card ruled him out of the 1990 World Cup Final made him a national icon. Missed penalties from Chris Waddle and Stuart Pearce made the booking a technicality – but Gazza's elevation to superstardom could not be stopped.

INVENTION OF THE WORLD WIDE WEB

@TimBernersLee
I just implemented the first successful
communication between a Hypertext Transfer
Protocol (HTTP) client and server. Happy Xmas, y'all!
3.12pm, December 25, 1990

@PeopleOfBritain
STFU – we're watching @QueenLiz2's speech!
3.13pm, December 25, 1990

@TimBernersLee
You don't understand – this prototype offers
WYSIWYG browsing/authoring!
3.14pm, December 25, 1990

@PeopleOfBritain
Snoooooorrrrrrrrreeeeeeeeeeeeeeee...
3.16pm, December 25, 1990

@GaryGlitter
Just had a peek at this internet thing. Hats off to
@TimBernersLee – a true game-changer.
4.21am, December 28, 1990
[Retweeted by @ChrisLangham & way too many
others.]

The World Wide Web sprang into life on
Christmas Day, 1990. It has been a force for good
(and the not so good) ever since.

THE IRAQ WAR (PART 1)

@SaddamHussein
Just mooched into Kuwait. #AndItFeelsSoGood
10.11pm, August 2, 1990

@GeorgeBush
@SaddamHussein See you there, dude #gameon
9.30am, January 16, 1991

@SaddamHussein
@GeorgeBush Oh, scared. #Not
9.33am, January 16, 1991

@GeorgeBush
We've got @SaddamHussein's ass out of Kuwait.
#swag
10.10pm, February 28, 1991

@SaddamHussein
@GeorgeBush But you didn't finish me off,
did you? #inoffthered
10.11pm, February 28, 1991

@GeorgeBush
@SaddamHussein @Dubya Heck, you gotta leave
something for your boy.
10.14pm, February 28, 1991

*The first Gulf War, fought in 1991, saw the Allies
remove Saddam Hussein's army from Kuwait.*

THE QUEEN'S ANNUS HORRIBILIS

@QueenLiz2
Gosh, @Prince Andrew and @Fergie are going to
split up. At least there aren't any
#embarrassingfergiephotos or wotnot.
12.11pm, March 19, 1992

@QueenLiz2
Now @PrincessAnne is getting divorced. Oh well,
onwards and upwards.
11.12pm, April 23, 1992

@AndrewMorton
Proud to be publishing *Diana: Her True Story*
today.
9.00am, June 16, 1992

@QueenLiz2
Shit. #embarrassingfergiephotos
8.44am, August 1, 1992

@QueenLiz2
Blast, Windsor Castle is on fire. Worried one will
have to doss the night at a hotel in Slough or
somesuch.
8.12pm, November 20, 1992

@PrinceCharles
@QueenLiz2 Ma, sorry to break it to you this way,
but @Diana and I are getting divorced.
5.59am, December 9, 1992

@QueenLiz2
Can one get #AnnusHorribilis trending?
6.01am, December 9, 1992

The monarchy was rarely amused during 1992.

TORY SLEAZE

@AntoniaDeSancha
#FF @DavidMellor – because he's soooo powerful
and beautiful...
11.12am, September 25, 1992

@DavidMellor
@AntoniaDeSancha Beautiful? Me? You'll be
telling me @JohnMajor's a player, next!
11.13am, September 25, 1992

@EdwinaCurrie
@DavidMellor @AntoniaDeSancha Well, now you
mention it...
11.16am, September 25, 1992

@TimYeo
@JohnMajor Boss, you know the whole
#backtobasics campaign? Problem: I've got my
mistress up the duff. Happy Xmas, anyway!
11.51pm, December 24, 1993

@JohnMajor
Fuck me. At least it can't get any worse...
6.02am, December 24, 1993

@StephenMilligan
Wearing ladies' underwear & stockings? Check.
Electric flex around neck? Check. Poppers-soaked
orange in my mouth? Check. Ok - party time!
8.40pm, February 8, 1994

@MohammedAlFayed
DM to @NeilHamilton
Did you get the brown envelope? Make sure you
ask that question for Big Mo.
5.12am, 2 October, 1994

@JeffreyArcher
Won't Tweet for a while as I'm orf to prison. It's
my choice to go to jail. I'm happy about it. Honest.
I've been to Mars. Twice. Seriously.
4.22pm, August 9, 2001

*During the 1990s the Conservative Party was hit
by a succession of scandals. Despite leader John
Major's efforts to promote family values as part of
a 'back to basics' drive, his MPs continued to
embarrass him and the party, to the amusement
of a nation.*

GEORGE GALLOWAY & SADDAM HUSSEIN

@GeorgeGalloway
#FF @SaddamHussein I salute his courage, his strength, his indefatigability.
11.11am, July 11, 1994

@SaddamHussein
@GeorgeGalloway Thanks dude. Means a lot.
11.18am, July 11, 1994

@GeorgeGalloway
@SaddamHussein You're welcome, sir. Would you like me...to be the cat?
11.19am, July 11, 1994

@SaddamHussein
@GeorgeGalloway Steady on old boy!
11.29am, July 11, 1994

George Galloway's fawning praise for Iraqi dictator Saddam Hussein has haunted him almost as much as his cat impersonation in Celebrity Big Brother.

GOD, ATHEISM AND ALL THAT

@JoanOsborne
What if god was one of us?
7.11pm, March 30, 1995

@TonyBlair
@JoanOsborne What – just a slob like one of us?
#prezza
5.12am, May 3, 1997

@AlastairCampbell
DM to @TonyBlair We don't do god
5.13am, May 3, 1997

@JoanOsborne
Just a stranger on the bus, trying to make his way
home...
5.14am, May 3, 1997

@RichardDawkins
Oh dear, the whole God delusion...
5.15am, May 3, 1997

@JoanOsborne

And yeah, yeah – god is great. yeah, yeah – god is good

5.17am, May 3, 1997

@Nietzsche

And no, no – god is dead. No, no – god is dead...

5.18am, May 3, 1997

@God

Oh for my sake!

5.19am, May 3, 1997

Is atheism the new religion? Some think so.

HARRY POTTER

@JKRowling

Bored on the train.

5.55pm, June 1, 1990

@JKRowling

Still bored on the train.

6.24pm, June 1, 1990

@JKRowling

Idea: how about a story about a geeky kid with glasses who becomes a wizard and battles a dark wizard? RT if you like it.

6.29pm, June 1, 1990

[Retweeted by 450m users]

Bored on a long train journey, JK Rowling found that an idea for a fantasy novel 'fell into her head'. It turned out to be a rather successful idea.

THE DEATH OF DIANA

@HenriPaul

Sat bored alone in a hotel bar.

8:02pm, August 30, 1997

@HenriPaul

Drunken Tweeting FTW!

9.45pm, August 30, 1997

@HenriPaul

giong to go forr a drriev. BRB.

11.40pm, August 30, 1997

@TonyBlair
She was the people's princess and that's how she
will stay, how she will remain in our hearts and in
our memories forever.
8.14am, August 31, 1997

@BritishPublic
@ThePress You're disGUSting! We're un-following
you...once we've bought your commemorative
supplements
7.12am, September 1, 1997

@RollingNewsBroadcast
Now, the latest on the death of Diana...she's still
dead.
11.47pm, September 4, 1997

@Elton'sEyebrows
Going to grab an early night. Big day for us at
Westminster Abbey tomoz.
8.31pm, September 5, 1997

@EarlSpencer
@Elton'sEyebrows And for moi...
11.40am, September 6, 1997

@PaulBurrell

In 1993, @PrincessDi DMed me: 'My husband is planning "an accident" in my car...in order to make the path clear for him to marry.'
7.11am, December1, 2007

@MoFayed

Psssst...plot MI5...MI6...mumble...crocodile wife...Phillip Frankenstein...Roswell...is Elvis even dead...mumble grumble...passport...
11.11am, February 18, 2008

Diana, Princess of Wales died in a car crash in Paris in August 1997. A week of mourning followed during which anger erupted against the press and the royal family. Conspiracy theories about the circumstances of her death have continued ever since.

THE MILLENNIUM DOME

@TonyBlair

Sorry, but I'm genius – I just had an awesome idea. Anyone know how easy it is to build a dome? Can't be hard, right?
04.02am, 2 June, 1997

@TonyBlair

Game on. It'll be a triumph of confidence over
cynicism, boldness over blandness, excellence over
mediocrity – and all that for just £758m!
10.02am, 12 July, 1997

@PrinceOfDarkness

Thanks for giving me the #dome gig, I'll deliver
big-time – just you wait. Love, Mandy xoxo
10.03am, 12 July, 1997

@TonyBlair

@PrinceOfDarkness How are we getting on with
the #dome? @CherieB and me are hoping to throw
a big bash on millennium eve...
4.23pm, 29 November, 1999

@PrinceOfDarkness

@TonyBlair Stop getting your knickers in a twist!
10.21am, 30 November, 1999

@TonyBlair

@PrinceOfDarkness Erm, rich coming from you.
You do know it's meant for *this* millennium
eve, right?
10.22am, 30 November, 1999

'Pressing the *send* button on your first day is a classic mistake.'

@PrinceOfDarkness
@TonyBlair Hahahahahahahahaha – as if!
10.23am, 30 November, 1999

The Millennium Dome, intended to be a
triumphant symbol for the start of the third
millennium was instead regarded as an expensive
and embarrassing fiasco. Nowadays it hosts the
far more successful O2 Arena.

BILL CLINTON AND MONICA LEWINSKY

@BillClinton
I did not have sexual relations with that woman
8:02pm, January 26, 1998

@BillClinton
#TheAwkwardMomentWhen I admit that indeed I
did have a relationship with Miss Lewinsky that
was not appropriate
7:42pm, August 17, 1998

President Bill Clinton admitted having a
relationship with former White House intern
Monica Lewinsky following a four-year inquiry
headed by independent prosecutor Kenneth Starr.

Clinton had previously strongly denied the allegation.

RON DAVIES' MOMENT(S) OF MADNESS

@RonDavies
Just going on a late-night stroll on Clapham Common with a dreadlocked man I just met. No biggie.
11.48pm, October 26, 1998

@RonDavies
Oh. It turns out that gay guys meet there for sex. Who knew?
4.12am, October 27, 1998

@RonDavies
Going to go badger-watching tonight. Apparently there's a great place just off the M4 near Bath.
11.59pm, March 1, 2003

@RonDavies
Oh. It turns out that gay guys meet there for sex as well. Who knew?
3.12am, March 2, 2003

*Who knew indeed. What a run of coincidences
Ron Davies MP has suffered from.*

THE *HEAT* ERA

@DaveandVicBecks
We don't like the attention that comes with fame.
Please RT
3:34pm, March 2, 1999

Heat *magazine was launched in 1999, shortly
before reality television shows such as* Big Brother
and Popstars *launched a new era in entertainment
and celebrity. The public has become sceptical of
some celebrities, including those who complain
about the pressures of fame while desperately
striving to cling-on to it.*

#FAMOUSLASTTWEETS (PART FIVE)

@RodHull
Watching Man Utd v Inter. The TV reception is
awful. Going to go up on the roof to fix it.
8:02pm, March 17, 1999

@Emu

Sob, booo hooo, sob...why...WHY?

5.12am, March 18, 1999

*The entertainer Rod Hull died while adjusting the
television aerial on his roof, mid-way through a
Champions League tie.*

THE SEPTEMBER 11 ATTACKS

@OssieBinL

Twitter's shit. I don't get any 'mentions' anymore.
And who does a guy need to screw to get some
followers?

11:00pm, September 10, 2001

@OssieBinL

Up at the crack of, here. No particular reason. Just
a normal day. Okay?

05:12am, September 11, 2001

@GeorgeWBush

Off to a school in Florida. They're going to teach
me how to read, or something.

6.01am, September 11, 2001

@GeorgeWBush
Apparently a plane has crashed into the WTC.
That's got to be a terrible pilot.
8.47am, September 11, 2001

@GeorgeWBush
SHIT.
9.04am, September 11, 2001

@OssieBinL
My 'mentions' are going wild. Won't be able to
reply to you all, nor return any #FFs for a while.
Actually, I might not Tweet for a bit.
10:04am, September 11, 2001

*On September 11, 2001, Al Qaeda terrorists used
hijacked airliners to attack American cities. Nearly
3,000 people died.*

POP IDOL

@GarethGates
My name is...my name is...my name is...
7.12pm, October 1, 2001

@Eminem
@GarethGates Dude, I've already written that one
7.13pm, October 1, 2001

@CarolineBuckley
Young man...it's fun to stay at the YYYYMCA!
7.14pm, October 1, 2001

@SimonCowell
I have heard some bad performances in my time.
And I can honestly say that is one of the worst
of them.
7.15pm, October 1, 2001

@GarethGates
My name is...my name is...my name is...
7.32pm, October 1, 2001

@SimonCowell
I don't mean to be rude, but you look like the
Incredible Hulk's wife
7.34pm, October 1, 2001

@Darius
Can you (still) feel the love in the room?
8.12pm, November 28, 2001

@SimonCowell

Butlins, yes. *Pop Idol*, no.

7.59pm, December 2, 2001

@GarethGates

My name is...my name is...my name is...

8.12pm, December 2, 2001

@SimonCowell

Distinctly average, I'm afraid

8.33pm, January 12, 2002

@WillYoung

@SimonCowell Don't be such a rotter. I don't think you could ever call that average. Unfollowed!

8.34pm, January 12, 2002

The first series of Pop Idol *was not the first reality talent contest but it was the first involving Simon Cowell. He never looked back.*

GUANTANAMO BAY

@Pentagon

@GeorgeWBush So dude, what are we going to do

with these here terrorists we've started catching?
12.12pm, January 11, 2002

@GeorgeWBush
@Pentagon Take 'em to Cuba and make 'em wear bright orange outfits. That'll learn the sonsofbiyatches.
9.00am, January 21, 2002

@Pentagon
@GeorgeWBush Mr President, that sounds like a holiday camp. Isn't there anything harsher we can do?
9.02am, January 21, 2002

@GeorgeWBush
@Pentagon We could, like, torture them? You know, strangle them, waterboard them, stick lit cigarettes in their ears, bash their heads in...
9.09am, January 21, 2002

@GeorgeWBush
@Pentagon What I mean is we *could* do that, but we won't. D'ya get me? We WON'T do that. Nudge-nudge wink-wink. *Coughs*.
9.10am, January 21, 2002

@Pentagon
@GeorgeWBush You got it!
9.11am, January 21, 2002

@BarackObama
I'm different. Vote for me and I'll shut
Guantanamo Bay. Immediately.
#theaudacityofhope
7.12pm, November 17, 2008

@BarackObama
Meh, I was just pissing about when I said that.
You know how it is. #theaudacityofhype
4.50pm, April 3, 2012

*Guantanamo Bay, a detention camp opened in
Cuba after the September 11 attacks, has been a
thorn in the side of terrorists – and, to an extent,
US presidents – ever since.*

THE IRAQ WAR (PART TWO)

@TonyBlair
#FF @GeorgeWBush – you should see the DMs he's
been sending me about WMDS in Iraq #terrifying
09:32am, September 12, 2001

@GeorgeWBush
@Tony Blair – that's ma boy!
05:04am, March 20, 2003

*Following the September 11 attacks on America,
President George W Bush beat the drum for war
on Iraq. His closest overseas ally was British Prime
Minister Tony Blair. They never did find those
weapons of mass destruction.*

CHERIE BLAIR

@CherieBlair
#weallgotthatonefriend who introduces us to
homeopathic dowser healers and conmen who
help us buy property in Bristol. Right?
3.01am, November 1, 2002

@CherieBlair
Oh. Just me then.
4.56am, November 1, 2002

@PiersMorgan
@CherieBlair How is that 'moral compass' coming
along, Chezza? PS – I've got more Twitter
followers than you!
6.47am, November 1, 2002

Cherie Blair hit the headlines in 2002 due to her relationship with controversial 'lifestyle guru' Carole Caplin.

THE BOJO YEARS

@BoJo
'How to cover-up extra-marital affairs'
9.12pm, 21 June 21, 2004

@BoJo
Oh blast – I thought this was Google!
9.13pm, 21 June 21, 2004

@BoJo
Putting a jolly good editorial in tomorrow's *Spectator*, about how mawkish Liverpudlians are.
10.12pm, October 8, 2004

@MacKenzieKelvin
@BoJo LOL – good luck with that, old boy.
10.13pm, October 8, 2004

@BoJo
It seems Boris hath been a naughty boy again. But

all I said was they have orgies of cannibalism in
Papua New Guinea! Must be more careful.
9.13pm, September 19, 2006

@BoJo
Portsmouth, eh? Full of drugs, obesity,
underachievement and Labour MPs!
10.45am, April 10, 2007

@BoJo
Oh dear...
10.46am, April 10, 2007

@BoJo
#FF @HelenMacintyre You should see her little
baby's hair – a wonderful unruly mop!
0.46am, November 7, 2010

@BoJo
Oh. Gosh. You don't think...Oh no, not again!
10.47am, November 7, 2010

*With regular gaffes, some romantic affairs and
other headline-grabbing moments, Boris Johnson
has kept the British public entertained for years.
He has also been a Conservative MP and London
Mayor.*

CHAV PANIC

@DailyExpress
Chavs are the new terrorists (who were themselves the new dangerous dogs). WE MUST STOP THEM!
6.00am, 1 May, 2005

@BluewaterShoppingCentre
This is terrifying! – There's nothing else for it – we're banning hoods from our premises.
9.00am, 1 May, 2005

@KentMonk
I was just got flung out of my local shopping mall - anyone know what that's about?
11.11am, 1 May, 2005

@DavidCameron
Like everyone else, I'm terrified of chavs. I've got the answer: We should all hug a hoodie.
2.02pm, 2 May, 2005

@DavidCameron
Ah. Apparently 'Hug A Hoodie' is the name of a gay porn film. To clarify: I wasn't suggesting that sort of thing.
2.03pm, 2 May, 2005

@DavidCameron
Not that there's anything wrong with that. But, look, we do need to do something about happy slapping.
2.04pm, 2 May, 2005

@DavidCameron
Right. I see. Apparently there's a 'risqué' film called *Happy Slapping*, too. Dear me, a man can hardly open his mouth these days.
2.05pm, 2 May, 2005

@DavidCameron
What dirty minds you have. All I'm saying is that we need to discipline wayward youths. Perhaps it's time to bring back spanking?
2.09pm, 2 May, 2005

@DavidCameron
Let's drop it.
2.10pm, 2 May, 2005

Scare stories about the white working-class caused panic and posturing in the 21st century. Newspapers, retailers and politicians alike jumped on the bandwagon.

'It's not exactly ROFLcopter...how about trying a novel?'

THE RISE OF ENVIRONMENTALISM

@AlGore
Listen people, we have to reduce energy consumption at home NOW or @ThePlanet is going to blow up! #AnInconvenientTruth
04.00am, May 1, 2006

@ThePlanet
OK, @AlGore how about you cut your energy consumption at home? It's 20 times the national average! #heatedswimmingpool #electricgate
04.01am, May 1, 2006

@AlGore
@ThePlanet Gimme a break – nobody's perfect...
04.02am, May 1, 2006

@ThePlanet
True, @AlGore. Anyway, don't let us stop you from private-jetting around the world to tell everyone to...stop jetting round the world.
04.03am, May 1, 2006

@TrudieStyler
@ThePlanet It's not easy being a green campaigner! Anyway, off to a party tonight so I'm

flying my hairdresser from New York by private jet.
5.01pm, May 12, 2009

@PrinceCharles
One is flying to Copenhagen to give a speech at a
climate change conference. Flying back three
hours later. Thank goodness for private jets!
7.12am, 14 December 2009

@PrinceCharles
Taking the Royal train on a nationwide tour for a
week to promote how important cycling is for the
environment. #livestrong
11.12am, September 4, 2010

@JohnTravolta
@PrinceCharles Adaboy! We all need to do our bit
for climate change...as I was telling the pilot of
one of the five private jets I own.
11.13am, September 4, 2010

@ThePlanet
With friends like these...
11.17am, September 4, 2010

*Environmentalism became increasingly popular
and fashionable in the 21st century. Not all the
campaigners were as sincere as they could be.*

WHAT TONY DID NEXT

@TonyBlair
Resigned as PM today. Looking for new work. CV:
bombed Iraq and Afghanistan. Any offers?
4.44pm, June 24, 2007

@TheUN
Fancy becoming Middle East Peace Envoy?
8.44am, 27 June, 2007

@TonyBlair
@TheUN Erm, I assume you're taking the piss?
8.45am, 27 June, 2007

@TheUN
@TonyBlair Nope, quite serious.
8.47am, 27 June, 2007

@TonyBlair
Fuck me...
8.49am, 27 June, 2007

*Many felt there was a certain irony in Tony Blair
becoming an envoy for Middle East peace. Not
least lots of people in the Middle East.*

WHAT CHERYL DID NEXT

@CherylCole
I beat-up a black woman in a toilet, me marriage
to football's most hated man has failed & me
band's seen better days. What next?
10.02pm, May 30, 2008

@SimonCowell
@CherylCole Hello you...
10.02pm, May 30, 2008

*Cheryl (formerly Cheryl Tweedy and Cheryl Cole)
was offered X Factor salvation by Simon Cowell. It
all worked beautifully... until they tried the same
trick in America.*

SARAH PALIN

@SarahPalin
Honoured that @JohnMcCain has chosen me as his
running mate. Can't wait to become the Deputy
co-Prime President of Romania!
11.34pm, August 29, 2008

@SarahPalin

Discovered a great thing today – newspapers. You should check 'em out – they have photos and everything. Which do I read? I read 'em all!

4.44am, September 1, 2008

@SarahPalin

Foreign policy is my speciality – you can see Russia from my house in Alaska. And I'm telling ya, we gotta stick by our North Korean allies!

2.12am, September 4, 2008

@SarahPalin

Just got asked what my view on gay marriage is. I dunno, I don't buy into all that climate change shizzle. Put that in your pinko pipe!

2.34am, September 5, 2008

@SarahPalin

Can't wait for the #AmericanIdol final. Vote for me and @JohnMcCain because we've got #TheXFactor. We gonna kick JFK's ass!

2.34am, September 5, 2008

@SarahPalin

What are my views on the credit crunch? I'm here to talk about politics not pop music.

#KeepingItReal

2.35am, September 5, 2008

@SarahPalin
In an interview. The dude asked me for my
intellectual heroes. I said George Dubya, Ronnie
McD and Jabba The Hut.
11.11am, September 6, 2008

@SarahPalin
Apparently I need five, though. Can you think of
one more?
11.12am, September 6, 2008

@JohnMcCain
Sorry I've not been on Twitter for a while, been
busy campaigning. What have I missed?
4.13pm, September 6, 2008

@JohnMcCain
Oh. Shit.
4.14pm, September 6, 2008

*When John McCain chose Sarah Palin as his
running mate for the 2008 American Presidential
elections he had no idea what an impact she
would make.*

SADDAM HUSSEIN EXECUTED

@IraqiJudge

Hey @SaddamH, you used to kill Iraqi people - and
now Iraqi people are going to kill you. Isn't it ironic?
06.00am, December 30, 2006

@SaddamHussein

@IraqiJudge Totally – it's like raaaa-aaiiin on your
wedding day, it's a free ride when you've already
paid...
06.01am, December 30, 2006

*Saddam Hussein was executed by hanging after
being found guilty of crimes against humanity
following a year-long trial.*

THE INVENTION OF THE IPOD

@SteveJobs

I'm pretty stoked to unveil the iPod. You can now
carry your entire music collection in your pocket.
09.30am, October 23, 2001

AlanSugar

@SteveJobs That'll never work. By next Christmas
the iPod will be dead, finished, gone, kaput.
You're fired!
09.31am, February1, 2005

@SteveJobs

@AlanSugar Dude, we totally just sold our
300millionth iPod.
05.28pm, October 04, 2008

@AlanSugar Are there any programmes that
deleet old Tweets?
05.29pm, October 04, 2008

@PiersMorgan

RT @AlanSugar Are there any programmes that
deleet old Tweets? <–- It's 'delete'
05.34pm, October 04, 2008

@SteveJobs

@PiersMorgan Lol!
05.35pm, October 04, 2008

*The Apple iPod, the best known of MP3 players,
was launched in October 2001. Alan Sugar
predicted that it would be short and unsuccessful
fad. The sales figures proved otherwise.*

OSAMA BIN LADEN ASSASSINATED

@OssieBinL
Just moved into a new gaff. I'm loving it! We're
safe as houses with these here walls.
4.59pm, May 10, 2006

@OssieBinL
Must say, I'm likin' the look of this
@BarackObama dude. If @GeorgeW couldn't catch
me this dude never will. Nice name, too.
4.12 am, November 5, 2008

@USNavySeals
How ya doin, @OssieBinL?
01.03am, May 02, 2011
[Retweeted by @BarackObama]

@BarackObama
Ladies and gentlemen, @OssieBinL sleeps with
the fishes
9.00 am, May 02, 2011

*Al-Qaeda leader Osama Bin Laden had been living
in a compound near Islamabad in Pakistan for five
years when US Navy Seals burst in and
assassinated him. He was quickly buried at sea.*

TIGER'S TRYSTS

@NationalEnquirer
@TigerWoods Is it true you've been having an affair?
8.42pm, November 20, 2009

@TigerWoods
@NationalEnquirer Excuse me? As if I, a married man, would ever sleep with some rando. Can you even imadge?
8.44pm, November 20, 2009

@TigerWoods
Totally just had a minor collision in my Cadillac SUV. Hit a fire hydrant, a tree and several hedges. No biggie – just standard 2am stuff.
2.52am, November 27, 2009

@TigerWoods
Oh, I was bleeding and semi-conscious, too. As I say, no biggie. I'm a family man. Quit with the unfounded rumours!
2.59am, November 27, 2009

@TigerWoods
Shit.
2.11pm, December 2, 2009

@TigerWoods

I've let my family down & I regret those transgressions with all my heart. I've not been true to my values & behaviour my family deserves
5.12pm, December 2, 2009

@TigerWoods

I'm far from perfect. Somewhere between 12 & 120 affairs away from perfect. I'll survive: I'll just confess in a self-righteous styleeee.
8.44pm, November 20, 2009

Tiger Woods fiercely denied having extra marital affairs until the combined force of a 2am car crash and a leaked voicemail showed otherwise. He then embarked on a peculiar PR drive to try and redress the damage to his image.

THE 2010 GENERAL ELECTION

@GordonBrown

@LabourAide Who the *fuck* was that bigoted woman?
11.51am, April 28, 2010
[Retweeted by @SkyNews and 56million others]

@GordonBrown
@LabourAide Was that a Tweet? I thought it was a DM. Ach, bollocks to it!
11.52am, April 28, 2010

@NickClegg
Guys: vote for us and we will scrap tuition fees, oppose a rise in VAT and protect the National Health Service. #promise
23.59pm, May 5, 2010

@NickClegg
Sorry, I meant: vote for us and we will not scrap tuition fees, not oppose a rise in VAT and not protect the National Health Service. #mybad
9.00am, May 7, 2010

@DavidCameron
Good chap, @NickClegg. Now remember what I said: we all take you jolly seriously – you've even got your own ministerial car! *pats head*
9.01am, May 7, 2010

The 2010 general election delivered a hung parliament. David Cameron's Conservatives formed a coalition government with Nick Clegg's Liberal Democrats.

PHONE HACKING: PART ONE

@SteveCoogan
Come on, @HughGrant, we need to nail these
tabloid ogres. We can't take this lying down!
22.59pm, July 2, 2010

@HughGrant
@SteveCoogan Now come-come old bean. I've
taken a bit lying down in LA.
11.21pm, July 2, 2010

@PiersMorgan
@SteveCoogan @HughGrant I've got more Twitter
followers than you!!!
11.25pm, July 2, 2010

@MaxMosley
@SteveCoogan Could you 'block' me on Twitter?
I'm happy to pay for the displeasure...
11.51pm, July 2, 2010

@SteveCoogan
Pack it up, Mosley. I'm tired of this vulgarity.
We've got a crusade to launch here. I'm thinking
Richard the Lionheart!
12.01am, July 3, 2010

@HughGrant
Reminds me, @Hugh'sAgent do you think I'll be able to play Hugh Grant in Leveson: The Movie? #anyonebutcoogan
12.03am, July 3, 2010

@SteveCoogan
Why won't you take this seriously? I'm talking about a crusade for decency, sincerity and truthfulness!
12.04am, July 3, 2010

@PeterStringfellow
@SteveCoogan Mr Coogan, you know we have a 'no-tweeting' policy at @Stringfellows
12.16am, July 3, 2010

To be continued....

SOMEONE LIKE ADELE

@OfficialAdele
Popping round to see my ex. I heard he's married now. It's out of the blue. He hasn't invited me. Hope he sees that for me it isn't over.
4.44pm, August 19, 2010

Adele has shown that heartbreak can pay. She's now worth £20m.

BERLUSCONI'S BONKING

@SilvioBerl
#sinceimbeinghonest I've had a hair transplant, plastic surgery and I wear built-up heels to make me look taller.
1.12am, October 12, 2010

@SilvioBerl
But, come on, you'd do the same if you were hiring topless young hookers to come to your #bungabunga parties!
1.13am, October 12, 2010

@SilvioBerl
Oh, it turns out I fucked-up our economy, too.
1.17am, October 12, 2010

@AngelaMerkel
@SilvioBerl Zis is disgusting behaviour. You've got a veel pvoblem!
4.42pm, September 14, 2010

'Unfortunately illuminating the strike placards could take a few years.'

@SilvioBerl

@AngelaMerkel Yeah, and you've got an un-fuckable fat arse, love!

4.43pm, September 14, 2010

@AngelaMerkel

@SilvioBerl Uffffffffff!!!!!!

4.44pm, September 14, 2010

Despite being engulfed with political and personal scandal, Silvio Berlusconi served three terms as Prime Minister of Italy.

JOEY BARTON ARRIVES ON TWITTER

@Joey7Barton

People think I'm just a thug but I'm actually a philosopher. I want to use Twitter to show how deep I am.

2.11am, October 2, 2010

@Joey7Barton

For instance, as Benjamin Franklin said: anyone who trades liberty for security deserves a slap in the face.

2.14am, October 2, 2010

@Joey7Barton

Then there's Nietzsche. He said God is dead. And so will you be if you look at me funny, by the way.
2.17am, October 2, 2010

@Joey7Barton

It was Plato that said necessity is the mother of invention. Start on my Mum and I'll put you in hospital.
4.44am, October 2, 2010

@Joey7Barton

I was reading Freud earlier: 'If youth knew; if age could.' Me? I'll take you all on.
1.11am, October 5, 2010

@Joey7Barton

Lots of disagreement here. Well, even a clock that does not work is right twice a day. Fuck the lot of you.
2.14am, October 5, 2010

Part philosopher, part footballer, part convict, Joey Barton is arguably Twitter's finest figure.

KIM JONG-IL DIES

@KimJongIl
On a train. Soooooo bored. I could die of boredom.
Lol, hope this doesn't turn out to be one of them
#famouslasttweets!
3.12pm, December 17, 2011

North Korean dictator Kim Jong-il died while
sitting on a train near Pyongyang.

WORLD POPULATION REACHES SEVEN BILLION

@UnitedNations
Tomorrow, the world's population will reach seven
billion. Can we get a RT?
7.52am, October 31, 2011
[Retweeted by @BabyNargis and 6999999999 others]

The United Nations estimated that on October 31,
2011, the world's population reached seven
billion. A baby girl called Nargis, born in India that
morning, was unofficially named as the seven
billionth person.

THE 2012 BUDGET & U-TURNS

@GeorgeOsborne
We're imposing a VAT rise on Cornish pasties and caravans. And get this: there's nothing you can do to stop it. Arf arf!
2.12pm, March 21, 2012

@DavidCameron
Actually, change of plan. Ignore previous Tweet.
(cc @GeorgeOsborne)
9.12am, June 1, 2012

@GeorgeOsborne
Fine! But to everyone taking the piss about this, we are NOT a government prone to u-turns!
9.17am, June 1, 2012

@GeorgeOsborne
Well, apart from on buzzard nests, secret courts, the Euro veto, jobs law reform, sentencing, joint strike fighter, health reform...
9.20am, June 1, 2012

@GeorgeOsborne
...forest sell-offs, state retirement age for women, rape anonymity, milk cuts, bookstart funding,

housing benefit cuts, circus animal bans
9.22am, June 1, 2012

@GeorgeOsborne
Knife crime sentencing, domestic violence
protection orders, snap school inspections, child
benefit, NHS targets, charity tax & petrol duty
9.23am, June 1, 2012

@GeorgeOsborne
APART from those, we are an entirely decisive
government!
9.24am, June 1, 2012

@DavidCameron
@GeorgeOsborne Actually, G, can we take another
look at that plan to offer tax relief to the
computer games industry?
9.25am, June 1, 2012

@GeorgeOsborne
Uffffffffffffffffffff!
9.27am, June 1, 2012

@DavidCameron
@GeorgeOsborne Chillax, dude.
9.28am, June 1, 2012

The coalition government has proven less averse to u-turns than Margaret Thatcher was...

LADY GAGA RULES TWITTER

@LadyGaga
Hi, it's Monday today.
3.20pm, March 5, 2012
[Retweeted by @GagaAboutGaga and 20million others]

@GagaAboutGaga
@LadyGaga OMG! OMG! OMG! That's SO true – it IS Monday today. GENIUS!
3.21pm, March 5, 2012

Lady Gaga reached 20 million followers in March 2012, confirming her status as the Queen of Twitter.

PHONE HACKING: PART TWO

@RobertJay
Just got up. Time to trim and style the beard for breakfast.
8.12am, April 2, 2012

@RobertJay
Breakfast was lush. Now, time to tackle the beard for the day.
8.44am, April 2, 2012

@RobertJay
Done that. Memo to self: darling, you look sen-sational. Off to work now.
8.49am, April 2, 2012

@RobertJay
Proceedings start shortly. Just time for a quick check of the beard.
9.55am, April 2, 2012

@RobertJay
I think I made a real impact today and, furthermore, I think we all know why. Speaking of which, back in five...
6.12pm, April 2, 2012

@SamanthaBrick

@RobertJay Do you find you get a lot of jealousy because of your beard? Does it make other men envious?

11.11pm, April 2, 2012

@RobertJay

@SamanthaBrick All the time, darling, all the time. BRB.

11.14pm, April 2, 2012

With his neatly trimmed beard and yellow-rimmed glasses, Robert Jay QC was one of the Leveson inquiry's most colourful characters.

THE KONY VIDEO

@JosephKony

Just joined Twitter. How do I get followers?

7.52am, October 31, 2011

@JosephKony

I don't even know if I'm going to bother with Twitter any more. I never get any mentions.

7.52am, October 31, 2011

@JosephKony
Fuck – @JustinBieber tweets one video of me and suddenly I've got millions of mentions. Must watch the video later, see what it's all about!
7.52am, October 31, 2011

@JosephKony
Shit just got serious. Laters.
7.52am, October 31, 2011

A 30-minute campaign video about Ugandan warlord Joseph Kony went viral in March 2012. It brought his story to 50 million people in just four days thanks to RTs from celebrities including pop star and Twitter king Justin Bieber.

PHONE HACKING: PART THREE

@TomWatson
Rupert Murdoch: unfit to run a company.
4.44pm, May 1, 2012

@RupertMurdoch
@TomWatson: unfit to get up the stairs.
4.44pm, May 1, 2012

@TomWatson
Alex Ferguson: unfit to manage a Premier League
football club.
4.45pm, May 1, 2012

@TomWatson
iPhones: a flawed business model from a no-good
two-bob company
4.46pm, May 1, 2012

@TomWatson
China: nobody lives there.
4.47pm, May 1, 2012

@TomWatson
Justin Bieber: an obscure nobody
4.48pm, May 1, 2012

@TomWatson
The Romans: what did they ever do for us?
4.49pm, May 1, 2012

@TomWatson
Me: brave, audacious and humble campaigner. I'm
totes amazeballs.
4.49pm, May 1, 2012

Tom Watson, fresh from newspaper exposure over his expenses scandal, spearheaded attempts to bring down Rupert Murdoch.

THE GREAT BRITISH DROUGHT OF 2012

@WaterBoards
We are now in drought. Hosepipes are now banned. £1,000 fine if we catch you using one.
5.01, April 2, 2012

@WeatherPeople
Weather forecast for first-half of April: Rain. All day. Every day.
5.02, April 2, 2012

@EnvironmentAgency
We've issued 30 flood warnings.
9.12am, April 13, 2012

@WaterBoards
Reminder we are in drought. Hosepipes are now banned. £1,000 fine if we catch you using one.
9.12am, April 13, 2012

@WeatherPeople
Weather forecast for second-half of April: Rain.
Heavy rain. All day. Every day.
8.12pm, April 15, 2012

@EnvironmentAgency
Unprecedented rain has caused several areas of
Britain to flood.
5.12pm, April 19, 2012

@WaterBoards
Reminder we are in drought. Hosepipes are now
banned. £1,000 fine if we catch you using one.
5.13pm, April 19, 2012

@WeatherPeople
Weather forecast for first-half of May: Rain.
Heavy rain. All day. Every day.
9.01am, May 1, 2012

@WaterBoards
Reminder we are in drought. Hosepipes are now
banned. £1,000 fine if we catch you using one.
9.02am, May 1, 2012

@TheBritishPeople
WT actual F?
9.04am, May 1, 2012

*Endless, torrential rain and flooding in a country
technically in drought - only in England?*

AUSTERITY (PART ONE)

@DavidCameron
@GeorgeOsborne I say, Gideon, are you any good
yourself at wallpapering?
12.51pm, May 13, 2012

@GeorgeOsborne
@DavidCameron Why? Do you need Number 10
doing again? I told you, get the scum to pay for it.
12.52pm, May 13, 2012

@DavidCameron
@GeorgeOsborne No, I'm just wondering what
we'll do when the whole politics thing collapses in
front of us.
12.53pm, May 13, 2012

@RebekahBrooks
@DavidCameron You could go back into PR?
12.55pm, May 13, 2012

@DavidCameron
@RebekahBrooks LOL
12.57pm, May 13, 2012

To be continued, one suspects...

AND ONE FROM THE FUTURE...

@LastManStanding
Quite funny to think now that we all thought it
would be the environment or a nuclear war that
would end the world, when it turned out to be
09.00am, January 1, 2013

@LastManStanding
Damn that 140-character limit!
09.01am, January 1, 2013

@God
Launches Earth 2.0
09.02am, January 1, 2013

THE TWITTER MANIFESTO

To be banned from Twitter:

1. Public sector workers
2. Anyone from Scotland
3. People who explicitly ask celebrities for an 'RT'
4. Fat people (see 2)
5. Tweeters who cannot make their point in 130 characters or less. (In these times of austerity we're going to need those 10 characters back...)
6. Anyone who sends rude Tweets to Piers Morgan
7. Anyone who sends polite Tweets to Piers Morgan
8. People who apologise 'for not Tweeting' after a mere one-day Twitter silence
9. MPs whose first name is Tom and surname is Watson
10. Anyone who has time to Tweet more than once a week